Recovery
— FROM THE —
SOCIOPATH

Recovery
— FROM THE —
SOCIOPATH

After the antisocial,
narcissist or psychopath,
how to rebuild your life

DONNA ANDERSEN

Anderly Publishing
Egg Harbor Township, New Jersey

Back cover photography by Bill Horin

Anderly Publishing
3121-D Fire Road, #304
Egg Harbor Township, NJ 08234 USA
www.anderlypublishing.com

Library of Congress Control Number: 2020932410
ISBN: 978-1-951347-06-2

First softcover edition February 2020

Contents

Introduction

The sociopath has taken a wrecking ball to your life. Emotionally and psychologically, you're depleted. You've lost money, your job, your home, your friends and family, or all of the above.

Some people may be advising you to just, "put it behind you." Unfortunately, it's not that easy. Betrayal by a sociopath shakes you to your core. The practical aspects of rebuilding your life may seem insurmountable. You may be suffering from anxiety, depression, post-traumatic stress disorder, and/or a myriad of physical illnesses. You may wonder if it's even possible to recover.

Yes, it is.

Recovery from the devastation of a sociopath is a three-step process:

1. **Understand what happened.** This means educating yourself about what sociopaths want, how they behave and how they reel you in.
2. **Make the decision to heal.** Yes, you've been pummeled by a self-serving, manipulative sociopath. But you can choose to pull yourself out of the experience and reclaim your life.
3. **Do the emotional work.** True recovery comes from processing the emotional wounds of the sociopath's betrayal, along with any prior wounds that made you vulnerable to the sociopath in the first place.

This book, in fact, all of the books in the *Best of the Lovefraud Blog* series, will help you get started. I know, because it's the process I used, and I've seen it work for others.

I met and married a man, James Alwyn Montgomery, who turned out to be a sociopath. He took $227,000 from me, cheated with multiple women during our short, two-year marriage, had a child with one of the women, then married her, while still married to me. It was the second time he committed bigamy.

When I finally learned the truth of my relationship — that my husband never loved me, he just wanted my money — I was crushed. I felt like a fool. I didn't know how I was going to climb out of the hole.

But I did. About a year after my divorce in 2000, I met a wonderful man, and we've been together ever since. He supported my efforts to help others, and in 2005, after we got married, we launched Lovefraud.com to help people recognize and recover from sociopaths.

And what exactly is a sociopath? You may think they are all criminals and serial killers — many people do. But the original meaning of the term, when it was coined by psychologist George E. Partridge in 1930, was, "anything deviated or pathological in social relations."

Today the word "sociopath" is no longer an official clinical diagnosis. Instead, mental health professionals use the diagnoses of antisocial, narcissistic, borderline, histrionic or psychopathic personality disorders.

On Lovefraud, I use the word "sociopath" as it was originally intended — as an umbrella term for people who are maladjusted in their relations with others and society, and motivated towards antisocial behavior. I define a sociopath as a person with a serious personality disorder in which he or she manipulates and exploits others.

Best of the Lovefraud Blog series

I've been writing about sociopaths for years now, and Lovefraud.com has more than 4,000 blog posts. With so much content, it can be difficult to find articles on particular topics. Therefore,

Introduction

in this *Best of the Lovefraud Blog* series of books, I've collected, updated and organized hundreds of posts into specific themes:

- *Understanding the Sociopath*
- *Seduced by a Sociopath*
- *Dealing with a Sociopath*
- *Recovery from the Sociopath*

The articles are short, which will help you if you're working through trauma due to your experience with a sociopath. *Recovery from a Sociopath* offers advice, suggestions and encouragement in bite-sized pieces. Yes, recovery is possible, and I hope these articles will help you to overcome your experience, and move on to the life you truly want and deserve.

5 steps to recovery from the sociopath (they're not fast or easy, but the healing is real)

Finally, you realize what is wrong with your romantic partner: He or she is a sociopath.

Finally, the behavior that was so confusing makes sense. The person you loved, and who you thought loved you, has a personality disorder. Now you realize that anything your partner told you could have been a lie. Now you know why your partner could be so cruel, then tell you how much he or she loved you, practically in the same breath. Now you realize that there never was any love, that your entire relationship was exploitation, and nothing more.

Now what do you do? How do you move forward? How do you recover?

Many of your friends and family tell you, "Just put it behind you. Get over it. Move on." You are particularly likely to hear this advice if you were "only" dating the person, not married.

The friends and family dispensing this pithy advice probably were never involved with a sociopath. They don't understand the depth of the betrayal. When you split from a sociopath, it is not a normal breakup. The intensity of these relationships makes the end incredibly painful.

Here are five steps for true recovery. This process is not instant, and it will likely be painful, but a new, much healthier you is waiting on the other side.

1. Understand that this relationship is an addiction

The sociopath initiated this intensity in the beginning of the relationship by showering you with attention, wanting to be with you all the time, claiming that you were soul mates, and painting a glimmering picture of your future together. You, never having experienced such adoration, believed that he or she was head over heels in love with you. Even if you felt misgivings, you suppressed them and focused on the promise of happily ever after.

Then, sooner or later, the sociopath did something to make you feel fear or anxiety. Perhaps you caught your partner lying or cheating. Perhaps he or she suddenly became enraged — you weren't sure why — and threatened to end your relationship.

Whatever it was, the bliss that you felt in the beginning was shattered, and you wanted it back. You asked what was wrong, tried to work things out, perhaps even apologized for something that you didn't do. Eventually the sociopath relented, and you kissed and made up.

Then, the whole cycle started again: Intense attraction. An incident causing fear and anxiety. Relief. Around and around it went.

This process has a profound psychological effect — it actually makes you addicted to the relationship. That's why it's so hard to break up with a sociopath. You're not breaking off a relationship — you're breaking an addiction.

2. Choose yourself

Addictions don't just go away. Anyone who has quit smoking, drinking, drugs or any other addiction knows that it's hard work. You must choose yourself, your health and wellbeing, over the addiction. Then you must work on your recovery, day in and day out.

A relationship with a sociopath is the same. You cannot simply "put it behind you." You cannot fully recover by locking your devastation into an internal closet, never to be opened, while attempting to go through the motions of living. If you try to do this, you simply end up with an emotional cancer within you, eating away at your life force.

The solution is to choose yourself. Make a commitment to yourself that you will recover, and then work it, day by day.

3. No Contact

The first step is No Contact. Get the person out of your life.

17

Stop seeing and talking to him or her. Block emails and text messages. Don't visit his or her Facebook page.

This will be difficult in the beginning, because, remember, you are breaking an addiction. You'll feel a compulsion to contact your former romantic partner. But if you do, it's just like an alcoholic falling off the wagon. You'll be back at square one, and you'll have to start the recovery process all over again.

The secret to breaking the addiction, as they say in 12-step programs, is to take it one day at a time. So commit to yourself that you will not contact the sociopath today. Then you make the same commitment tomorrow, and then the next day.

The longer you stay away from the sociopath, the stronger you become.

4. Deeper healing

Getting the sociopath out of your life is only the first part of your recovery. The second, and most important part, is healing whatever made you vulnerable to the sociopath in the first place.

We all have vulnerabilities — it's part of being human. We have internal fears, doubts and injuries from our past. Or we have dreams and ambitions — these, too, in the practiced hands of a sociopath, can become vulnerabilities, when he or she promises to make them come true. But generally, the sociopaths target our weaknesses, because that's the easiest and most effective way to hook us.

Usually the weaknesses boil down to a subconscious belief, deep within us, that we are not good enough.

We rationalize that our mother ignored us, or our father abused us, because we were not good enough. We assume that an earlier romantic involvement failed because we were not good enough. These ideas may have been deeply buried, but they still caused pain, and pain created vulnerability. Sociopaths can sense vulnerability like a shark senses blood in the water.

5. Releasing the pain

How do you recover from these deep wounds? You acknowledge that they exist. You look at them and allow yourself to feel the associated emotions — pain, disappointment, fear, anger, rage, numbness — and then you let the emotions go.

This is a process, and is best done in private, or with the help of a competent therapist. You'll find that you have layers and layers of pain, and as you release one, another rises to take its place. You may find yourself crying, wailing or stomping to release anger. You work your way through the layers of emotions, acknowledging, feeling and releasing.

You can't do this all at once — it's too draining, and you still have to live your life. In fact, you should intersperse these sessions of releasing with times of treating yourself well, and feeling joy at whatever goodness you experience, no matter how small.

True recovery isn't easy, fun or instant — it takes work and a commitment to yourself. But the rewards are so wonderful: Release from old traumas. Life lived with peace and lightness. The opportunity for true love and happiness.

It all begins with making a decision to recover.

How to implement No Contact

When you realize that that you are involved with a sociopath, the standard advice from Lovefraud is that you should, as quickly as possible, cut the predator out of your life. That means no phone calls, no emails, no texts, and certainly no in-person meetings. It means No Contact.

Of course, there are times when this is difficult, such as when you work with the sociopath, or you have children together. In these cases, you need to implement No Contact as best you can. But let's now talk about situations where it is possible to get rid of the person, such as in a dating relationship.

What is the best way to establish No Contact? Clearly, firmly and permanently.

The rules of No Contact

The book called *The Gift of Fear,* by Gavin de Becker, devotes several pages to the topic of rejecting an unwanted suitor, and these pages are among the most helpful of the entire book.

De Becker writes in the context of a woman who decides she doesn't want to be involved with a man. Do not, the author says, try to "let him down easy." Here's what he writes:

> One rule applies to all types of unwanted pursuit: Do not negotiate. Once a woman has made the decision that she doesn't want a relationship with a particular man, it needs to be said one time, explicitly. Almost any contact after that rejection will be seen as negotiation ... If you tell

someone 10 times that you don't want to talk to him, you are talking to him nine times more than you wanted to.

Here are more points that de Becker makes in the book:

- If you get 30 messages from a pursuer, and finally call him back to say, "stop calling," he learns that after 30 attempts, he will get a response.
- If you make an excuse like, "I don't want to be in a relationship right now," the stalker assumes you will want to be in a relationship later, and keeps calling.
- If you say, "You're a great guy, but I'm not the one for you," the stalker thinks you're just confused, and will come around in time.
- Never explain why you don't want a relationship. If you give a reason, it gives him something to challenge.
- A nice or delicate rejection is often taken as affection.

"The way to stop contact is to stop contact," de Becker says. "I suggest one explicit rejection and after that absolutely no contact. If you call the pursuer back, or agree to meet, or send him a note, or have somebody warn him off, you buy another six weeks of his unwanted pursuit."

Giving in

What happens if you're wishy-washy about No Contact? Lovefraud received the following letter from a reader whom we'll call "Lenore."

I literally had to count the days that went by as I refused contact with him, and on day 120, I celebrated because I felt healed. Well, on day 121, he emailed me, and against my better judgment, I emailed him back. He told me he had been in therapy, he realized what he had done wrong, he was on medication.

I was cautious and wary, and decided, amidst warnings of concern from my friends and family, to perhaps work on a friendship again. We worked on being friends for a few weeks, and everything was great and fine. I felt in control of the situation.

Then his old behaviors started creeping in. He installed a GPS app on my phone so he could track my whereabouts. He began calling and texting incessantly, and flipping out if I didn't answer right away. The verbal and psychological abuse had begun again. Fortunately, this time it did not escalate to physical abuse. He began lying again, gaslighting and acting erratically, and began seeing other women on the side. Last night, it once again became too much and I told him not to contact me again because my heart and my spirit couldn't take any more pain, and his inconsistency is so bad for my son.

So today begins Day One again without him. I am writing you today to tell you that your no contact advice was the best advice I didn't take. For 120 days I went without him. It took a while, but by day 90 I was happy and free and at peace. Now I am back to square one.

No Contact is the path to healing from an entanglement with a sociopath. The stronger you can be about No Contact, the faster you will recover.

7 steps to breaking emotional ties with a sociopath

If you're like most people who read Lovefraud, you may know, or suspect, that the person who is creating havoc in your life is a sociopath. Whether the offending individual is a romantic partner, parent, another family member or a friend, he or she checks all, or most of, the boxes of the sociopath checklist.

You know the individual is bad for your emotional and psychological health, your wallet, and perhaps your safety. Still, you struggle to break free.

Sometimes there are financial or legal issues that make it difficult to escape. But often the ties that bind are emotional.

Emotional bonds can be extremely powerful. This is understandable, because sociopaths are skilled at sinking their hooks deep into your head, heart and soul. Still, breaking the emotional ties will set you free. And if you can't totally escape — if you share children, for instance — breaking the emotional bonds will make it easier to cope.

Here are 7 steps to emotional escape:

1. Recognize that you are being used

Sociopaths live their lives by exploiting others. It's critical for you to understand that no matter what the individual says, or how much he or she cries, the objective is to keep you dishing up his or her narcissistic supply. The supply could be money, food, sex, a place to live, a job — whatever. The sociopath may even just be enjoying the entertainment of pulling strings and watching you jump. In any event, this is not a relationship of give and take. It's you give, and the sociopath takes.

2. Understand that the sociopath never loved you

The core of the sociopath's personality disorder is an inability to love. A key component of real love is caregiving — the motivation to take care of, support, and provide for the people you love. Sociopaths can't do it. They are literally missing the ability to put the good and welfare of other people before their own. Yes, they can fake it sometimes, especially while they're reeling you in. But any apparent actions to support you always have an ulterior motive. Despite the sociopath's flowery language about true love, destiny and soul mates, he or she never truly loved you. It is impossible.

3. Do not take it personally

You didn't do anything to deserve terrible treatment at the hands of the sociopath. All people, to a sociopath, are objects to be used. Sociopaths are exploiters and manipulators, and nothing you could have done would have made any difference. You were simply a convenient target. If the sociopath didn't do it to you, he or she would have done it to someone else. In fact, sooner or later, the next person who gets lured into the trap will also be abused.

4. Give up hope

Hope is a virtue — except when you are dealing with a sociopath. Remember: Once a sociopath is an adult, there is no rehabilitation. There are no drugs or therapy that can turn a sociopath into a kind, loving and honorable person. No matter how much the person pleads, no matter how much the person promises to go to therapy or church, do not believe that he or she will fundamentally change. Oh, you may see some temporary improvement — sociopaths can keep their nasty behavior under control when they want to, long enough to draw you back in. But sooner or later, the exploitation and manipulation will return. In fact, it will probably become worse.

5. Accept what happened

To break the emotional bonds, you need to admit — primarily to yourself — that the sociopath really did lie, cheat, steal, manipulate, abuse and assault. It was no accident. You did not imagine the bad behavior. No matter how much the sociopath tries to blame others, including you, everything that happened, did happen, and it was intentional.

Accepting what happened does not mean the sociopath's behavior is acceptable — far from it. Acceptance means that you no longer make excuses. You open your eyes to the truth, no matter how painful.

6. Decide that you are finished with the sociopath

You cannot wait for the sociopath to let you go. This person will never let you go as long as you are useful to him or her in some way. And you'd be amazed at what the sociopath considers to be useful — it could be that he or she just enjoys watching you squirm. Therefore, YOU must be the one to make the decision — your involvement is over.

7. No Contact

The first five steps are about really seeing and accepting the truth of your situation: You are being abused and exploited, the sociopath knows exactly what he or she is doing, and it will never get better. In the sixth step, you are gearing up to make a change.

The seventh step — No Contact — is action. You cut the person out of your life. You do not see the sociopath in person, you do not talk on the phone, you do not respond to emails or text messages, you do not visit his or her Facebook page. If you are forced to have contact with the person — perhaps because you share children — any communication is strictly business, and you implement No Contact everywhere else.

No Contact is what enables the emotional ties to unwind and dissolve. The longer you stay away, the more the fog in your brain will clear, your heart will heal and your strength will return.

In fact, when you feel better, you may start to think that you can be "friends" with the sociopath. No, you can't. If you allow

25

yourself to have any communication with the person, he or she will latch onto you, you'll feel the emotional ties again, and you'll have to start the process all over.

No Contact is forever. And with that, you will be free.

Releasing the pain inflicted by a sociopath

Lovefraud heard from Janine in Florida. Here is what she wrote:

> In May it will be two years since I realized my ex-husband was a sociopath and every day I deal with the psychological nightmare that he has given me. I try so hard not to think about the destruction he has done to me...but every day it is there. Destroyed period.
>
> How can one put this behind them?? Yes I have moved on with my life — but every day in my mind what he did to me is there and will be in my brain forever. I have been told to forgive him and I do in a way because I realize how sick he is — but it is still there!
>
> Taken, abused, used, destroyed as a woman, as a human being and of course him shoving everything down my throat. Defaming my character, slandering me and doing his best to destroy my life. That is the hardest part, the man I helped the most in my life to live his dreams became my nightmare...I will carry this with me until my dying day.

Sociopaths charm their way into our lives, destroy us, and then leave. They go on their merry ways, and we are left with emotional train wrecks. Anger, shock, betrayal, disbelief, disappointment, sadness, shame, fear, grief, hatred, rage — all adding up to

27

incredible pain. What are we to do with it?

I believe we must allow ourselves to feel it.

Facing the Fire

In 1993, I attended a workshop given by John Lee, author of *Facing the Fire: Experiencing and Expressing Anger Appropriately.* Lee talks about anger as a physical sensation that gets stuck in the body. Many of us walk around carrying decades of anger—childhood anger at our parents, anger from adolescent taunts, anger from previous husbands or wives. Unless we do something about it, the anger of the past stays there, affecting our present.

Anger builds into rage. Rage builds into numbness.

John Lee's book offers techniques for dealing with our anger. Many of us try to intellectualize our anger away. This doesn't work. Anger is a physical emotion that needs to be physically released. The idea is to do it without hurting other people or domestic animals. Lee suggests pounding pillows, twisting towels, stomping on the ground and breaking old cups and saucers into trash cans. We have to keep doing it until we experience a release.

Experiencing the pain

When I finally learned that my ex-husband was a con man, that he had fathered a child with another woman during our marriage, that the $227,000 he took from me was gone, I had extreme anger — and all of those other negative emotions — adding up to incredible pain.

Luckily, I had employed John Lee's techniques before — I tried them all, and found that punching pillows worked best for me. I also had a therapist who guided me in experiencing my pain. Because that is what needed to happen.

The pain had to come out, and the way to do it was physically. This meant punching pillows until I collapsed. It meant crying — deep, loud wails. It meant telling my ex-husband, emphatically, exactly how I felt — even though he wasn't there to hear it.

Make no mistake, this is not pretty. It is best done in privacy, or with a skilled therapist. And it takes a long time, because there are layers and layers of pain—you dig one out, and another one surfaces.

But it works. I can honestly say that the pain is gone—not only the pain of the sociopath, but the pain I was carrying around beforehand that enabled me to fall for his lies.

I have recovered. I am happily remarried to a wonderful man. And I am peaceful.

How long does it take to recover from a sociopath?

When I talk to people who have had their hearts broken into a million pieces by a sociopath, a question that I'm frequently asked is, "How long does it take to recover?"

I wish there were an easy answer to the question, but there isn't. Involvements with sociopaths cause serious damage to our emotions, psychology, health, finances, social connections — to our very lives. What I can say is that recovery is certainly possible, but it will probably take longer than a typical breakup.

Not breakup — betrayal

Why is recovery from a sociopath so difficult? Because this is NOT a typical breakup — it is a profound betrayal.

When normal people enter into a romantic relationship, it's because we are searching for an authentic connection with another human being, a person to love, who will stay with us through thick and thin. Sometimes, we discover that the relationship just isn't working out. Perhaps our lifestyles are too different, or we live too far apart, or we can't tolerate each other's quirks. It's painful, in fact, one person may hurt more than the other, but we tried and failed.

With a sociopath, however, the entire premise of the relationship was a lie. The normal partner was looking for an authentic connection, but the sociopath was looking for someone to exploit. We discover that the sociopath just wanted money, or sex, or was living a double life, and all the sociopath's professions of love and promises for the future were just bait to keep us hooked.

The betrayal leaves us shaken to the core. Therefore, more time is necessary for us to get over it.

How much time? It's impossible to predict because every case is different. The short answer is that it will take as long as it takes — but there are steps you can take to make it go faster.

No Contact

First, and most important, have No Contact with the sociopath. Cut the person out of your life. No phone calls, text messages, email and certainly no in-person meetings. Why is this so important? Relationships with sociopaths change the structure and chemistry of your brain, much like addictions. In fact, many people experience these relationships as addictions. Therefore, you must break the addiction.

The longer you "stay on the wagon" and maintain No Contact, the stronger you become. This is using time to your advantage. But as anyone who's struggled with other types of addictions knows, if you give in to your addiction a little bit, you have to start all over again. The time you previously spent maintaining No Contact is lost.

In situations where you must have some type of contact, such as shared parenting, your goal is to do your best to minimize interactions. More importantly, you want to go for Emotional No Contact. This means you get to the point where the sociopath simply means nothing to you. You know and accept what the sociopath is, and when you see that typical behavior, you just roll your eyes.

Because No Contact is so important, it is one of the issues you need to consider when deciding whether or not to pursue holding the sociopath accountable for his or her actions. I believe sociopaths should be help accountable — they get away with their moral or actual crimes far too often, which emboldens them and harms society. But the truth is that going after the sociopath keeps you in contact with them, which can slow down your recovery. So you need to decide — is it worth it?

Hastening the recovery

The other thing that can make your recovery faster is consciously deciding that you are going to heal, and taking the necessary steps to do it.

First and foremost, take care of yourself — eat right, get exercise, get sleep, don't smoke, drink or do drugs. Involvement with a sociopath may have left you with anxiety or depression. Healthy habits go a long way towards combating anxiety and depression.

You then need to decide that you're going to deal with the emotional and psychological effects of the involvement, using whatever method works for you. If you can find a therapist who gets it — great. If you find comfort in church, prayer, meditation or spiritual practice — fabulous. I used both of these approaches — plus my personal favorite, pounding pillows in which I envisioned my ex-husband's face. However you do it, you must get the toxic emotions and energy out of your system, or they will eat you up.

I also believe it's important to look deep within ourselves, beyond the experience with the sociopath, to discover why we were susceptible to the sociopath in the first place. These human predators target our vulnerabilities. In fact, they can spot vulnerabilities that we don't even know we have.

Did we have wounds from our childhood? Did we have mistaken beliefs that we were unworthy or unlovable? Something made us vulnerable. To truly recover, we must find out what it was and heal it.

If we maintain No Contact with the sociopath and focus on our own healing, over time, recovery will happen. And sooner or later, we'll discover that our lives are happier than we ever thought they could be.

How childhood pain leads to involvements with sociopaths

Lovefraud recently received this letter from a woman whom we'll call "Nina." I'm posting Nina's story because many Lovefraud readers have told me of similar patterns in their lives.

I love this man like I've never loved before. He seemed to be my soul mate. I have had two failed marriages (no sex in them).

I was touched by a neighbour starting when I was 10 and it continued for eight years. My father was totally controlling and I was not allowed friends or to go anywhere except to this neighbour. Both were depressed parents and did not show affection, only criticism.

I have always felt alone but now am — parents dead, sister dead within last four years. I am 57.

I met him seven years ago and he was totally charming and enchanting.

He pursued me for 11 months before I let him kiss me, and a year before I let him "make love."

I have got myself totally embroiled in a situation with him and my life revolves around him. He has a partner now — his wife and seven other women that I know of.

He speaks to me in a terrible manner a lot and is demeaning and rude and cruel and thoughtless. Tells me he loves me all the time.

I can't understand why I find it ok to let him treat me

33

this way. I desperately want him to love me and can't imagine not having him in my life. Feels not worth living. We have good times together playing music and he is a good lover (I think, although I have nothing to compare). He doesn't know I know about most of his other women but he often has us crossing paths.

I don't want to lose what may be a relationship worth keeping, yet it causes me so much pain and torment I don't think it can be worth it.

He owns a huge property and I live in the same building paying rent. I help with any work that needs to be done, as my biggest dread is being on my own, so I work with him and his nephew.

I have myself totally tangled up with him. He sometimes seems such a caring man yet at other times a completely selfish one. Over these last six plus years I have let him become part of almost every bit of my life. I am trying to open other avenues, but have no family and no "true" friends.

I am trying to work out why it is so important to me to find out if he is a "sociopath," as really, how he treats me should be enough for me to say that I deserve better. I have worked really hard on improving myself for over 25 years now, and although I have come a huge way, I still feel very stuck in myself a lot.

My problem is I would become homeless, know nobody and my greatest fear is being alone and rejected — can't see a way out.

What is he — just a selfish, inconsiderate, narcissistic, thoughtless man, or am I too fussy? Sometimes he can be very nice and seems thoughtful.

Don't feel other option/s are worth considering — all feels hopeless and useless and impossible.

I feel when I tell what I've allowed that I am extremely stupid and weak.

Roots of the pain

Why is Nina in this situation? I believe the roots reach back to the beginning of her life, which she explained at the start of her letter. Nina says she endured:

- Depressed parents, who showed no affection, only criticism
- A controlling father, who wouldn't let her have friends
- Sexual assault by a neighbor from ages 10 to 18

After that, Nina had two failed marriages with no sex. So, as Nina says, she has "always felt alone." And even though her parents contributed mightily to her pain, they are now dead, so she truly is alone.

Seven years ago the man Nina writes about showed up. In the beginning he pursued her with charm and enchantment. After she finally agreed to a physical relationship with him, his treatment of her changed. Now Nina experiences:

- Cheating — the man has a wife and seven other women
- He is demeaning, rude, cruel and thoughtless, yet still says he loves her
- He arranges for Nina to cross paths with his other women
- They have sexual relations
- Nina pays the man rent and does work for him
- The man is entangled in all aspects of Nina's life

Cause and effect

I see a direct cause-and-effect relationship between Nina's past and the mistreatment she is now experiencing at the hands of the sociopath — and yes, he is a sociopath.

This man's level of disorder may be low- to mid-range — unless he's also doing other things that Nina hasn't mentioned. But he is definitely toying with her, cheating and taking advantage of her. The

35

guy is an exploiter, so in my book, he's a sociopath.

Nina's prior disappointments, betrayals and traumas primed Nina to be his target.

Hungry for love

Nina's parents did not provide her with love, so I believe she did not develop a solid understanding that she, like everyone, is worthy of love. Now she is hungry for any scraps of love she may find.

"I desperately want him to love me," she writes.

Inappropriate sexual contact

Nina was abused from age 10-18, and apparently her parents did nothing. (Her father may have even been complicit.) Nina then had two sexless marriages — which may have been her own reaction to the childhood abuse.

Then she meets the sociopath, who takes a year to get her into bed. Because of his diligent pursuit, Nina probably believed his intentions were sincere — after all, who chases someone for a year just to get laid? Well, sociopaths do — they enjoy the game.

To Nina, this sociopath seems like an accomplished lover. This may be true — many Lovefraud readers have said that the best sex they ever had was with the sociopath.

But that only covers the physical aspects of sex. Sociopaths are not capable of emotional connection, so that dimension is missing from the experience, although they can be good at faking it. But because Nina herself has not experienced healthy sex, she may not realize what it can be.

Fear of being alone

Nina says that she always felt alone. This likely resulted from the lack of warmth in her home when she was growing up, and the fact that her father would not let her develop outside relationships.

Now Nina's family is gone, and she's living in a building owned by the sociopath. If she wanted to end the involvement, she would probably have to move. Nina didn't explain much about that situation, except that she fears being homeless.

Psychological love bonds

All of these issues created psychological vulnerabilities for Nina. And how do sociopaths hook their targets? They find psychological vulnerabilities and exploit them. One way they do this is by hijacking the normal bonding process. When two people become a couple, a psychological love bond forms between them. Intimacy, both emotional and physical, causes oxytocin to be released in the brain, which creates feelings of attachment. This is all normal.

But sociopaths then create fear and anxiety in their partners, perhaps by cheating or threatening to leave the relationship. Surprisingly, this has the effect of making the psychological love bond stronger. The target wants the relationship to go back to the happy days of the beginning, and may beg, plead and appease to make it happen. Sociopaths may be willing to go along with this, if it suits their purpose at the time. So if the two kiss and make up, the bond is strengthened again.

Intermittent reinforcement

Another technique that keeps the target attached to the sociopath is intermittent reinforcement. This is classic psychology — if laboratory rats don't know when pressing a bar will result in a food pellet, they keep pressing and pressing and pressing. The compulsion to engage in the behavior gets stronger and stronger.

Likewise, if Nina never knows when the sociopath is going to respond to her with affection, she keeps trying and trying. Any time he responds with affection, it reinforces her efforts and strengthens the compulsion she feels.

Tolerating bad treatment

Nina writes that she can't understand why she allows the man to treat her badly. It's because she has psychological vulnerabilities created by her family of origin and her prior experiences. The sociopath found and targeted those vulnerabilities.

Nina has experienced a lifetime of pain. The sociopath presented himself as the antidote to her pain. The love he expressed was fake, but Nina didn't know that, so she became emotionally and psychologically entangled.

Now she feels like she has no choice but to tolerate his bad treatment. In fact, she questions whether she is being "too fussy." This may be a psychological defense mechanism. Since she can't change him, she may subconsciously hope that changing her own expectations will make her feel better so she can stay in the relationship.

Except that the relationship is not healthy. Nina, like all of us, is deserving of love. Real, honest love. She's never going to get it from this man.

Full recovery

Nina's story demonstrates a big reason why sociopaths come into our lives: to help us recover from a lifetime of pain.

Involvements with sociopaths are bad. Really bad. They are so bad that, unlike other painful experiences we may have had earlier in our lives, the devastation of the sociopath cannot be ignored. We have to face it, or we'll fall apart.

If we examine the experience with the sociopath, we can often see that it is linked to previous life experiences. So to truly recover, we need to overcome not only the injury and pain caused by the sociopath, but the previous injuries and pain that made us vulnerable to the sociopath in the first place.

Then we can achieve real healing, and a life more brilliant than we ever imagined.

Nina's story clearly and concisely demonstrates how her past created an opening for the sociopath to exploit. I thank her for allowing me to share her story.

The next step for her, and for everyone with similar stories, is to address all the pain — both the recent experiences and the trauma from experiences long ago.

After the sociopath, consumed by obsession

The illusion is vaporized. One way or another, you have discovered that your partner, family member, friend or colleague is a sociopath. Maybe you unearthed one lie too many. Or maybe the mask slipped and the person unceremoniously dumped you. However it happened, you've learned that he or she has been lying to you all along.

And now you're obsessed.

You want to know the truth. You want to know where the sociopath really was, who the sociopath was really with, what happened to the money. With your new awareness of his or her lying personality, you recall multiple incidents that left you scratching your head, and now look at them in an entirely different light, trying to figure out what was really going on.

The sociopath is all you think about, morning, noon and night. You keep replaying incidents in your mind. You go back over old text messages and emails. You stalk the sociopath's Facebook, Twitter or other social media. You're desperate for answers.

And you wonder what's wrong with you.

Normal for survivors

First of all, after you've tangled with a sociopath, obsession is a normal part of the recovery process.

In her book, *Legal Abuse Syndrome*, Dr. Karin Huffer outlines eight steps to recovery from abuse — and believe me, deception and exploitation by a sociopath qualifies as abuse.

Step #3 is obsession. "Figuring out what happened and feeling a basis for feeling safe again preoccupies the victim's life," she writes.

This is why you are obsessed — your ability to perceive reality is critical to your sense of safety. The sociopath deceived you, so what you thought was reality turned out to be a shimmering mirage. Therefore, your sense of safety was shattered, and you want it back. You want to know what was real and what was fake.

No Contact

So obsession is a normal reaction to your experience — at least you know that you're not crazy. Still, it's unhealthy. Why? Because obsession interferes with No Contact.

No Contact means you cut the sociopath out of your life. You do not see this person, talk to them, exchange text messages or emails, or visit their Facebook page. When you go No Contact, the fog starts to lift and your mind starts to clear.

The goal of No Contact is to get to the point where you don't even think about the sociopath anymore. Well, if you're obsessing, you're thinking about the person, which is a form of being in contact.

What to do about obsession

On the one hand, obsession is normal. On the other hand, it interferes with your recovery. So what do you do?

You manage your obsession. Typically that means you set limitations on the time that you will allow yourself to think about the sociopath. Maybe you will permit yourself an hour a day in the beginning, with the goal of reducing the time as you move forward.

And what do you do for the remaining hours in the day when you want to obsess? You distract yourself. You find something else to occupy your time and your mind.

Maybe you'll watch movies on Netflix. Maybe you'll read an entire series of crime thrillers. One Lovefraud reader said that she worked on jigsaw puzzles. Physical activity of any kind is also a good idea. Create a new focus for your attention.

If you find yourself drifting off into obsession, pull yourself back and refocus. You also might want to consider EFT Tapping. This is a form of acupressure that breaks the connection between a memory and the emotional charge of the memory. Tapping on your experience with the sociopath will help decondition your brain to the obsessive responses.

For more information, see Lovefraud's webinars on EFT Tapping.

Obsession is a phase

The bottom line, therefore, is that obsession is a normal phase that you go through after you discover you've been betrayed by a sociopath. Instinctively, you are trying to figure out the truth, so that you can recover your sense of safety.

But the time comes when obsession interferes with your recovery. By managing the time that you spend obsessing, you can pass through the phase and move on with your life.

5 stages of endurance to help you recover from the sociopath

Sociopaths do terrible things to us. I hear so many painful stories from Lovefraud readers — perhaps you have a similar experience:

You may have had your heart shattered into a million pieces.

You may have lost your home, your job and all your money.

You may have suffered physical assault, illness, and emotional or psychological breakdown.

You who have lost your children, because the sociopaths got custody, poisoned the kids' minds, or both.

You may who have lost years of your life, time that can never be replaced.

Sometimes when I hear these stories, my heart just breaks. Because sometimes, as much as I would like to offer solutions, the sociopaths have enacted such total destruction that the chances of justice are very slim. The sad truth is that some of what was lost cannot be recovered.

When that's the case, for a while all you can really do is endure. But if you can keep enduring, it paves the way for recovery. Here's how:

Staying alive

The first stage of endurance is resolving to stay alive. I know from Lovefraud's surveys that about 30% of people involved with sociopaths feel so badly that they consider or attempt suicide. If you are in this dark place, ask for help. You may not be able to see it now, but you do have something to live for, whereas the sociopath will always be an empty shell. Do not give up.

The next step of staying alive is functioning. In the beginning, it may be all you can do to get out of bed. Make yourself get up and take care of your basic necessities. If you have a job, make yourself go to work, even if you have to go to the restroom frequently to compose yourself. Handle your responsibilities as best you can.

Yes, you may feel so numb that you are just going through the motions. But keep at it. Eventually the numbness will start the thaw, and then your recovery can begin.

Acceptance

The first step in recovery is acceptance. This does not mean that you are okay with what the sociopath did to you. It does mean that you accept the fact that the evil and destruction happened.

When you start to see the extent of the sociopath's betrayal, if you're like many people, you may be in denial. You want to believe the sociopath's words of love and reassurance, and not the truth of his or her actions. You may burn up a lot of emotional energy trying to find an excuse or a reasonable explanation for the sociopath's bad behavior.

Acceptance means realizing that yes, the sociopath hurt you; yes, it was on purpose; and no, the sociopath does not feel any remorse for what happened.

Emotional healing

This may seem counterintuitive, but your emotional recovery can begin even while the practical aspects of your life are in shambles. The key is choosing yourself, and deciding that you want to feel better.

How do you feel better? You give yourself permission to feel bad. Instead of trying to bottle up your internal turmoil, you allow yourself to feel the grief, sadness, disappointment, anger and pain.

This is not pretty — I spent hours curled up on the floor, crying. I also imagined my ex-husband's face on a pillow and beat it until I collapsed. If it helps, you can work with a therapist, or use techniques like EFT tapping. The objective is to process the emotions, so you can be free of them.

Letting go

To move into your future, you need to let go of the past. The money, house, job and whatever else you lost may be gone for good. You may have tried to seek justice through the law or the courts and failed, and it's time to give up the fight.

You may have to end certain relationships — certainly with the sociopath, but possibly with other friends, colleagues and relatives. You may even need to end contact with your own children.

Letting go means releasing your emotional attachment to what you wanted to happen. It means allowing yourself to move on. But sometimes, a funny thing happens when you let go. When time has passed and you're feeling better, some of what you wanted may actually transpire.

Wisdom

Although they are painful, entanglements with sociopaths are often valuable life lessons. You learn that some people can lie convincingly. You learn that some people have hidden agendas. You learn sociopaths exist — and now you know how to spot them.

You'll probably learn valuable lessons about yourself as well. Perhaps you believed that you deserved so little that the sociopath's lies and mistreatment were acceptable. Perhaps you now realize your parents or early romantic partners were disordered, and the damage they caused made you vulnerable to later predators.

You gain insight, and you can make future choices with wisdom.

Life changes. By enduring when things are really bad, we take incremental steps toward recovery. Then we let time work its magic. We probably won't be the same person who fell for the sociopath, but if we allow ourselves to heal, we can be stronger, smarter and healthier.

By enduring, we can recover, and then we may be surprised by the new opportunities life presents us.

12 reasons to forgive yourself for falling for the sociopath

Once I figured out that my entire relationship was a scam, the person I was most angry with was myself. I really beat myself up. Why did I fall for the lies? Why was I such a chump?

Sound familiar?

Since my disastrous experience with my sociopathic ex-husband, James Montgomery, one of the most important things that I've learned about tangling with sociopaths is that we shouldn't be so hard on ourselves for believing them.

We are not stupid. We are normal, empathetic people who didn't stand a chance against skilled predators, and here's a dozen reasons why:

1. No one told us about sociopaths. In school, church, college or even magazine articles, we never learned that there are people among us who seem to be normal but live their lives by exploiting others.

2. We are conditioned to be nonjudgmental and forgiving. All our lives we hear messages like, "we're all created equal" and "everyone deserves a second chance." No one says anything about exceptions to these platitudes.

3. We want to help people. We feel good when we offer assistance or do something nice for others. Sociopaths take advantage of this with their "pity plays."

4. Sociopaths are professional exploiters. They've been manipulating, lying and exploiting all their lives. They are very, very good at what they do.

5. Human beings are lousy lie detectors. Research has shown that people can spot a lie only about 53% of the time. That's not much better than flipping a coin.

6. The "warning signs" of lies do not work with sociopaths. They feel totally entitled to lie, so they do not exhibit any signs of distress or anxiety. That's why they can pass lie detector tests.

7. We are biologically programmed to trust people. Our bodies release a neurotransmitter called "oxytocin" when we experience intimacy — anything from a hug to conversation to sex. Oxytocin makes us trust people.

8. We all have vulnerabilities. A vulnerability means we want something. Sociopaths target our vulnerabilities by promising to give us what we deeply desire and to make our dreams come true.

9. Sociopaths hijack the human bonding system. They pour on the attention to make us feel close to them, and then they do something to make us feel fear and anxiety. This actually makes the psychological bond stronger.

10. We are not taught to trust our instincts. Usually we intuitively know that something is wrong with the person or the involvement fairly early on. But no one tells us to listen to our gut.

11. We're taught to give the benefit of the doubt. In the legal system, "everyone is innocent until proven guilty." We apply the same standard to our involvements, staying until we have proof. Then it's far too late.

12. We are normal people who have a heart and a conscience. And that's exactly what sociopaths use against us.

How to get revenge against a sociopath

You've finally figured out what is wrong with an individual who has taken advantage of you, abused you, perhaps even assaulted you. Reading Lovefraud, you realize that he or she is a sociopath.

Now, you're an emotional wreck. You've been profoundly betrayed. You're justifiably angry. Plus, the sociopath has caused you real problems. Perhaps all your money is gone. Or you're in a vicious child custody battle. You've lost your job, your savings or your home. You suffer from anxiety, depression or PTSD. You feel so far down that you don't even know which direction is up.

You are outraged by the sociopath's actions. You are further outraged that after this individual bulldozed through your life, he or she seems to be facing absolutely no consequences. The predator has simply moved on to a new target, leaving you in a heap of ashes.

You want your life back. You want the sociopath to be accountable for the destruction he or she caused. And you want to make sure he or she never does this to another human being. But the predator turns on the charm, or plays the victim, or convinces everyone that you are mentally unstable. No one seems to be able to help you. In fact, no one even understands what you're talking about.

It's infuriating. If you were honest with yourself, you'd have to admit that you really want revenge.

"Living well is the best revenge"

This proverb was recorded by the English poet George Herbert in 1651. Perhaps whoever originally said it hundreds of years ago knew about sociopaths.

Right now, with your life in tatters, you probably feel like "living well" is an impossible dream. But you can start working towards that goal immediately — and stick it to the sociopath in the process.

The sociopath's prime objective in life is power and control. If you deny the sociopath power and control over you, you take away what he or she wants most.

The power and control that the sociopath exerts is primarily over your thoughts and emotions. You can break that power and control, and it doesn't even have to cost you any money. The first step, of course, is No Contact. We talk about No Contact all the time on Lovefraud, but if you need a refresher course on how to do it, read *How to implement No Contact*.

It's true that No Contact is difficult in many cases, such as if you share children with the sociopath, or you work together. In these situations, you need to get to Emotional No Contact. That means you detach emotionally; you do not allow him or her to upset you. There are caveats to this as well, because sociopaths are capable of atrocious behavior that really pushes your buttons. In these cases, you certainly deserve to be upset — just don't let the sociopath see it.

Remember, they want power and control. If they see that they have triggered you, they know that they still have power and control over you.

The key, therefore, is to focus on healing yourself and improving your life. It will take time. It will require processing the pain, disappointment and anger of the betrayal. But if you decide to recover, you can do it.

This does not mean that the sociopath should get away with what happened. But if you want to hold the sociopath accountable, you need to do it from a position of strength. Working on your own recovery is the best way to develop the strength.

"Revenge is a dish best served cold"

The source of this statement is also unclear—it was first translated from French to English in 1846, but apparently was already a proverb by then.

It's not a good idea to consciously go out to seek revenge. (Another proverb attributed to the Chinese philosopher Confucius states, "Before you embark on a journey of revenge, dig two graves.") But as time goes by and you build your inner strength, you may suddenly find yourself faced with an opportunity to hold the sociopath accountable.

The sociopath, of course, will continue a life of destruction. Eventually, he or she may target the wrong person or seriously break the law, and someone may contact you to find out what you know about this disordered individual. Then, in a calm and collected manner, you can describe your experience, provide evidence that proves a pattern of behavior, and contribute to some type of justice — whether it's getting the individual prosecuted, exposed in the media, or just ruining his or her efforts with yet another potential victim.

Revenge may be possible, but probably not right away. So focus on your first priority, which is healing your own life. Then, be patient. By releasing the pain and upset of your betrayal, you'll be ready when an opportunity arrives for justice.

To you, justice will be sweet revenge.

If our emotions are triggered, there's more pain to process

Lovefraud recently received the following e-mail from a reader. We'll call her Sally.

It's been almost four years since I left my ex psychopath. He almost had me take my own life through guilt, when it was him lying, cheating, committing fraud, you name it — a textbook case.

The reason I write to you today, however, is I am so sad and disappointed in myself yet again. Four years and I thought I was over the damage done by the psychopath so I stepped out of my comfort zone to contact an old friend I had not seen since before the psychopath came into my life.

I made a decision to visit my male friend and we had a nice time. When I returned I started analysing the situation. Was my friend just after one thing? He had made a few small promises that had not come through (generally that wouldn't bother me too much). I felt like it was happening all over again. I felt cheated, lied to and manipulated by such minor matters.

The worst of all I let my friend have it by email. I was horrible, cruel and nasty; it was like my now lost friend was responsible for everything that happened four years ago just because he said a few things that he didn't come through with. So before I got hurt I lashed out and hurt him; I sabotaged something that could have been good in my life.

Now I just feel miserable. I was so nasty he will never speak to me again. I don't blame him. My underlying intention was to get that result. I really thought I had recovered; obviously not. Now I am scared I will never be able to recover.

Time and emotional processing

Recovery from an entanglement with a psychopath/sociopath takes both time and emotional processing. The operative word here is "both."

By emotional processing, I mean allowing ourselves to feel the deep disappointment, anger, hopelessness, rage, hatred — whatever painful emotions the involvement with the psychopath has generated within us. When we allow ourselves to feel these emotions — as uncomfortable as it is — when we are through, we can release them. The only way out is through.

Releasing the emotions is not an event; it's a journey. No one can know in advance how many times we will be dealing with painful emotions, or how long it will take to release them. The amount of emotional processing required, and the amount of time required, are different for every individual.

Sally's reaction

Sally's involvement with a psychopath was so damaging that she contemplated suicide. This is serious. She probably needs a lot of time and processing in order to recover. In fact, if she was willing to take the step of contacting the man, she's probably made a lot of progress.

Now, I can't tell if Sally's relationship with the man she contacted had the potential to be unhealthy. Was her intuition working, and the man was "just after one thing?" Or did she totally overreact?

The guy "made a few small promises that had not come through." This could be a red flag — if not of a psychopath, than of someone who is inconsiderate. And a relationship where one

51

party gets to be inconsiderate is at the very least, not fair to the other party. At worst, it could be the beginning of manipulation. So maybe Sally was justified in ditching the guy.

But she lashed out, and was then surprised and disappointed at the force of her own reaction. What happened? She experienced a "trigger." Something in her encounter with the man brought up more of the pain from her experience with the psychopath.

Always more to do

This means that Sally still has more emotional processing to do. There is still pain within her that needs to come out. It may be directly related to her experience with the psychopath. Or, it could be related to some other deep pain or disappointment she's carrying around — maybe from her childhood, or teenage years, or other relationships. I think Sally should view this incident as an opportunity for more healing, allow herself to experience the emotion, and release it.

If this man were truly a friend, Sally might be able to apologize, explain why she reacted the way she did, and he would understand and forgive her. But maybe the guy was a user and deserved whatever Sally said. If that's the case, she should just move on.

Yes, Sally has more work to do. And she's not alone.

In reality, we are never finished recovering. That's because, whether due to the psychopath or other disappointments in our lives, we're always carrying around some buried pain somewhere. But we can get to the point where the pain is minimal, and our lives are filled mostly with peace and joy. And that is the place we're all journeying to.

The sociopath's betrayal is not your life — it is an incident in your life

M any Lovefraud readers have experienced the phenomenon of "losing yourself" in the sociopathic relationship. Before meeting the sociopath, you may have been, for the most part, happy, confident, successful and financially stable. You had a network of people who cared about you. Yes, there was some kind of vulnerability — perhaps you were a bit lonely — and the sociopath used the vulnerability to infiltrate your life. But, for the most part, you were okay.

Then, either suddenly or slowly, your life disintegrated, and now the problems you face are so immense, and so interconnected, and so overwhelming, that you don't know where to begin unraveling them. You don't have the energy to start. Rather than the happy and confident person you once were, you are anxious, depressed and fearful. You don't know how you are going to survive.

And you don't know how it all happened. Trying to figure it out, you describe the individual's behavior to friends or a therapist, and someone mentions the word "sociopath." Or you do a Google search — perhaps on "pathological lying" — and end up on Lovefraud.

You are in shock. The description fits, and you realize that the individual never cared about you, that you were targeted, and that you allowed yourself to be scammed, either financially or emotionally. You've lost money, or your home, or your job, or your support network — or all of it.

Blame game

As you realize the depths of the betrayal, the blame game starts. And whom do you blame? Yourself.

You are furious with yourself for not seeing it sooner. You didn't listen to people who warned you, or to your own inner voice that was telling you something was amiss. Instead, you believed the silver-tongued liar, the crying and pleading actor, whose real intention was to drain from you everything he or she could.

Besides everything physical and financial that you lost, you are most upset because you no longer have your sense of self. You feel like you lost your soul.

Now what?

The sociopath is responsible

First of all, recognize that you are not responsible for the abuse you experienced.

The sociopath may have blamed you for his or her actions, saying, "You made me do it." Understand that statements like these were all part of the manipulation. The terrible words were spoken specifically to throw you off-balance and break you down, so that the sociopath could maintain control.

He or she is responsible for the hurtful words — and for all abusive actions.

Commit to recovery

Next, know that you can recover. The key to recovery is recognizing that the fraud and betrayal are NOT WHO YOU ARE. The devastation by the sociopath is something that happened to you. The betrayal was an incident, an experience. Do not allow it to define the rest of your life.

Make a decision, a commitment to yourself, that you are going to heal.

This means you need to allow yourself to experience the deep wells of pain, disappointment and grief that the experience caused. You have to get it out of your system, and the only way to do that is to allow yourself to process the pain, which means feeling it.

Finally, you need to let the experience go. How do you do this? You accept that it happened, and that there is nothing you can do to change the past. This does not mean you excuse what the sociopath did. But you do recognize that the betrayal was an INCIDENT IN YOUR LIFE, and NOT LET IT DEFINE THE REST OF YOUR LIFE.

It is true that you will never be the same after the experience with the sociopath, and you may have, in fact, lost yourself. But by facing the pain, processing it and letting it go, you can find a new "you," one with a richer, deeper understanding of the human condition, and more capacity for love and compassion than you ever had before.

You can recover. You can grow. You can acquire wisdom. And you can move on and find happiness — perhaps sharing the wisdom you acquired to help prevent others from going through what you experienced.

When women 'of a certain age' meet sociopaths

Editor's note: Lovefraud received the following email from a woman whom we'll call "Annamaria17." Donna Andersen responds below.

I met the SP in 2006 and he was a supervisor for electric utility company where I live. Due to a power outage he was the Environmental Rep and came to my home. He had just moved here from out of state and I immediately fell for him. We had lunch the next day and that was when I found out he was married. Unhappily of course.

Over the next few months, it was agonizing as he would disappear and I had already become addicted to him, the sex and everything else about him. Long story made short, he moved in with me and a month later a friend of mine disclosed that he was not only still seeing his wife, but had another girlfriend who lived nearby.

There was a 14-year age gap between us and I was living in a $1M home where he was living in a 1 room studio with his wife. He had no money, but I did and paid for everything.

Fast forward to 2009, he was transferred for work. Two months later he said he needed a break and I broke up with him, knowing that he wanted to be free of me to do other things I guess. We were soul mates, our birthdays were the same day and he would start a sentence and I'd finish it and the same for me. Everything was so perfect.

But, I was on antibiotics nearly the entire time we were together due to infections that he passed along. He would disappear for entire days at a time where I could not reach him. He would go on trips and never ask me to go along — aside from the fact I never really knew where he was going.

I loved him unconditionally though. He never mentioned the age gap and it never came between us.

But, when we broke up it was devastating to me. We spoke nearly every day (when I could find him) and then it went to nothing. I had never in my life had anything like that before.

Since then I have heard from him, but only for him to rub in the fact that now he was really happily married to someone else. He would ping my LinkedIn profile every month or so and I told him to stop. He kept it up until finally I called his employer and they got him to stop, with the threat that they'd call the police for stalking.

I'd like to add that we were both in counseling, and after he had left the area, I kept on. The therapist only told me a few years ago that the SP admitted to him that he was lying, not only to me on a consistent basis, but lied to the therapist as well.

So, with that said, I am still mourning over him and still cannot even look at his face on any social media (he is on all of them) without feeling like it was yesterday. I've not been able to date anyone else, it feels like I have 'loser' written all over me, or desperation.

Therefore, that is why I reached out to see if there was any type of literature that would help. I've left a lot out as there was so much more to say, but he lied about everything to me. I'd like to think that he cared at some point, or that he tried, but after all of this time I think that he never did. I also wonder if he is doing the same thing to his wife.

Are there any articles or information on relationships and the sociopath's effect on older women? I've been stuck for years and have never gotten over him. He, of course, has moved on, but I've not recovered. He was significantly younger than I, but I thought maybe there was something I could read on it?

Donna Andersen responds

I was 40 years old when I met my sociopathic ex-husband, James Montgomery. I had a successful career, made good money, but I had never been married. I was healthy, and I held out hope that I might yet have a chance for a family.

In other words, I was a nice, juicy target, primed for exploitation.

When sociopaths target women of a certain age — 40 or older — they have a very potent weapon to use against us: The fear that we're running out of time.

Whether it's a biological clock ticking so loudly that it can be heard in the next county, or we've endured a bad relationship and we're hoping to finally find a good one, or we had many wonderful years with a kind, loving partner and are now widowed, mature women can feel lonely and desperate. When sociopaths sense loneliness and desperation, they shout "Bingo!"

One reason why sociopaths target mature women is because we have assets. We have careers, businesses, homes, investments and retirement plans. My ex-husband took a quarter-million dollars from me. I've heard from other women who lost far more.

Lovefraud's research actually shows that people who meet sociopaths at a younger age — between 14 and 30 — suffer more harm. They suffer more physical abuse, lose more money, jobs and homes, and their lives are threatened more often. They also tend to stay in relationships with sociopaths longer — which means they eventually become mature women who have lost so much.

However we get there, mature women find ourselves with our lives half over, betrayed and devastated, and feeling like there's not much time to recoup and recover. It can lead to a sense of hopelessness.

So what can we do?

I think the key to turning our lives around is to take two profound truths to heart:

The past is gone, the future doesn't exist, and all we really have is the present moment.

It's not over until the fat lady sings.

Yes, the sociopath pretended to love us just so he could exploit us. Yes, it hurts. But as mature women, we can make up our minds to live our best lives in the present moment. This will make it possible for positive change to arrive in our future.

So to Annamaria17, I recommend that you make up your mind that you will do the emotional work necessary to recover from the sociopath. The first step is to go No Contact. I'm glad that you took action regarding your LinkedIn profile. But YOU must stop looking at his social media pages. YOU must block any further contact. (And yes, he is doing it to his wife.)

Remember that relationships with sociopaths are highly addictive, and it sounds like you are still feeling the addiction. We have plenty of information here on Lovefraud about No Contact and other steps you can take to recover. The key is making the decision to do it, and then following through, one day at a time.

As long as you're on this Earth, recovery is possible. Life can change. Opportunity may arrive at any moment.

I am living proof of that. I have been in a happy, healthy relationship with my new husband for 16 years.

3 steps to begin dating again after the sociopath

A reader posted the following comment on Lovefraud's Facebook page:

> This website helps me too, but now, as I venture into the world of dating again, I find that my past is terrible hindrance. So difficult. Any advice gratefully received. Just want to be happy.

Many times I've been asked, "After what your con artist ex-husband did to you, can you ever trust again?" Yes I can. I do. I am remarried, and I am happier now than I've ever been, in fact, I'm much happier than I ever was before the sociopath.

So how do you climb out of the abyss of profound betrayal? How do you recover? How do you move forward, to the point where you can actually love again?

Here are some lessons I've learned along the way. Maybe they'll help you.

1. The only way out of the pain is through it

It hurts. Once you finally realize that your entire relationship was a mirage, that there was no love, that the sociopath's intention all along was to exploit you, the pain is shattering. And, to make matters worse, you feel like a complete idiot for falling for the lies, for allowing the sociopath to take advantage of you as long as he or she did. Not only were you conned, but you participated in being conned.

You are filled with disappointment, despair, anger and outrage. You are totally justified in feeling these emotions, but they're really unpleasant. It's so painful, and you just wish it would all just go away. You may feel so overwhelmed that you ask a doctor to "give you something." But although antidepressants may help you cope in the beginning, when the shock is so raw, they don't solve the problem, they just mask it.

So sooner or later, if you want to recover, you need to face the pain head on. You have to get the toxic emotions out of your body, or they will eat you up. But you can't analyze yourself out of the pain. Emotion is physical, and it needs to be drained off physically.

The only real way to end the pain is to allow yourself to feel it. I spent many hours curled up on the floor, sunk into my grief. I screamed in rage. I envisioned my ex-husband's face on a pillow, and punched it until I collapsed.

Whatever technique you use to drain the emotion, you'll have to employ it more than once, because there isn't just one disappointment or one betrayal. Sociopathic relationships create layers of them, so getting rid of the negative emotion is a process. As you release a layer, another one will rise to the surface.

Here's the good news: Getting rid of the pain creates space within you to feel healthier emotions, like peace, happiness, gratitude and joy. The longer you travel down this path, the more the balance shifts. Your negative emotional state gradually transforms into a positive state.

I can't tell you how long it will take—everybody is different. But eventually, you can get to the point where you've released the pain. You don't forget what the sociopath did, but it just doesn't affect you any more.

It's best not to start dating until you've made good progress in dealing with the pain of the sociopath. If you try to meet someone while you're still wounded, there's a good chance that it will be another predator. He or she will seem to swoop in to rescue you, but the real agenda will be to take advantage of you — again.

Wait until you're feeling better before trying to date again.

2. Learn the core lesson

Sociopaths set out to exploit you, and they are fully responsible for the pain that they cause. Still, there was something within you that made you susceptible to the sociopath's charms and promises. Even when you felt misgivings, there was something that made you doubt yourself, listen to their explanations, give them another chance.

After this terrible betrayal, it's time for you to figure out what that original vulnerability was and heal it.

You may realize that you've experienced betrayal before. Perhaps your parents or other family members were disordered, and you grew up believing that manipulation and emotional blackmail were normal. Perhaps you experienced psychological, physical or sexual abuse, and never really recovered from those wounds.

Or maybe your parents did the best they could, but you still absorbed damaging beliefs. In my case, for example, I grew up believing that I wasn't good enough as I was; I had to earn love by being the "good girl" or getting all A's in school. Where did that idea come from? Well, perhaps from my parents. And maybe that's what they learned from their parents, who learned it from their parents. Mistaken ideas can be passed down from generation to generation.

It's time to break the chain.

Often, when you honestly examine the pain inflicted by the sociopath, you find that it is directly connected to some earlier, more hidden emotional or psychological injury. And that's when you may realize that you can draw value from the run-in with the sociopath. As you release the pain of betrayal, you can go deeper to release the pain of the original injury as well.

But it's important to be gentle with yourself. You didn't know about the deep injury, or to protect yourself, you pushed it out of your awareness. Now you need a shift in consciousness. Now it's time for you to believe that you are worthy, you are lovable, and you deserve the true gift of life, which is joy and happiness.

When you fully embrace these beliefs, you'll find your life experience matching them.

3. Trust your intuition

You may feel that after allowing yourself to become romantically involved with such a loser, you can't trust yourself to choose a healthy relationship. When you first end the relationship, this is probably true. That's why you shouldn't date right away. It's also why No Contact is so important — it gives you the time and space to psychologically disengage from the sociopath, so you can escape the fog of manipulation.

But as you travel the road to recovery, you'll become more comfortable believing in yourself, and trusting yourself. After all, you probably knew something was wrong with the sociopath, or the relationship, very early on. Most people do. But you didn't listen to your instincts, and continued the involvement until it turned into disaster.

Here is what you need to know: Your intuition is designed to protect you from predators. Your intuition is the best defense you have against exploiters. So if you ever have a bad feeling about someone, if you ever sense that something is off, pay attention.

Of course, sociopaths are really, really good at the game, so you may not pick up a warning right away. It may be weeks, or even months, before you see some WTF? behavior. But if you see that first hiccup, or become aware of that first little twinge of suspicion, tune into your own feelings. If you keep getting negative hits, act on your instincts and end the involvement.

Then, don't be upset that you attracted another one. Be proud that you caught on so quickly, before too much damage was done. It's a sign of your recovery.

The more you clear away the trauma, the better your intuition will work. Eventually, it will tell you that someone is right and good, and that it is safe to open your heart again.

And then, with all the healing work that you've done, you'll be able to experience true, fulfilling love.

Getting over the relationship that didn't exist

Lovefraud received the following email from a reader with important question:

> How do I process a relationship that had so many lies in it that I don't know really with whom I was involved?
>
> I miss the person I thought I knew so much, but at the same time, he was involved with someone else, and others, since at least last June. I thought he had had one affair — but not anything to the extent that it looks like now.
>
> How do I process a relationship I never had? Was he lying the whole time — acting out the "I love you's," the romantic comments, and the idea that we should be together? Is it all an act?

Most of us are reading and posting on Lovefraud because we were intensely, callously, brutally deceived in a relationship with a sociopath. The betrayal was so deep, and so profound, that all we can say is that the person we thought we knew, the relationship we thought we had, didn't exist.

Much has been written here on Lovefraud about the different aspects of recovery. But in response to this reader's email, I'll review some of the key points.

Understanding sociopaths and "love"

Sociopaths do not feel empathy for other human beings.

Therefore, they do not have the ability to love as we understand it. There is no emotional connection, no true caring for the target of their "affections."

What is going on when sociopaths say, "I love you?" They are not all the same, so there is a range of explanations for what they mean.

At the clueless end of the range, sociopaths may view the target as attractive arm candy, or may like the attention they receive from the target, or may enjoy sex with the target. Sociopaths may label as "love" whatever it is they feel with the target. So, "I love you" means, "I like how I look when you're with me," or, "I like the fact that you're showering me with attention," or, "I like having sex with you."

At the sinister end of the range, sociopaths know they are cold-hearted predators and view their targets the way cats view mice. These sociopaths play with their targets for awhile, then, when they tire of the game, abandon them, leaving the targets battered and gasping. Or, some sociopaths will go in for the kill, usually figuratively, but sometimes literally.

The reader asked, "Is it all an act?" Often, the answer is yes.

Accepting reality

The sociopath may have painted a picture of an exquisite future of unending togetherness and bliss. Or, the sociopath may have latched on to our own nurturing instincts, and convinced us that they can only survive with our caring and support. Then the mask slips, the story unravels, and we learn that everything we believed was a lie.

We must accept this reality. We must believe our own eyes and recognize the truth.

This may be really difficult. We thought we were working towards our dream. We made important life decisions based on what we were told. We may have spent a lot of money — maybe all of our money — at the behest of the sociopath.

We don't want to believe that it was all a cruel mirage. We argue with ourselves — there must be some other explanation, some other reason. We may say, "I must have misunderstood; no one can be that heartless."

Yes, sociopaths are that heartless.

The reasons they are heartless do not matter. Yes, in some cases they had bad parents and a terrible childhood. But as an adult, they are not going to change. They are what they are, and the sooner we accept that, the sooner we can begin to recover.

Time and permission to recover

The psychological and emotional damage that we suffer because of our entanglements with sociopaths is often extensive. We may experience anxiety, depression, guilt, self-hatred and perhaps even post-traumatic stress disorder.

Some of us are so angry with ourselves for falling for the scam that we punish ourselves by blocking our own recovery. We say we will never trust again, never love again.

Please do not feel this way. If you never recover, giving up on trust and love, the sociopath will have truly won. Deny him or her that victory. Give yourself permission to recover.

Recovering from this damage is not an event; it's a process. Readers often ask, "How long will it take?" The answer: It will take as long as it takes.

We may need to move forward in several directions at once, but it's okay to move forward slowly. Some steps to take:

- Protecting our physical safety, if the sociopath has made threats, and what remains of our financial assets.
- Taking care of our physical health — eating right, getting enough exercise and sleep, avoiding alcohol and other substances.
- Finding a way to release the pent-up anger and pain within us, without showing it to the sociopath, because that will backfire.
- Rebuilding relationships with family members and friends that were damaged because of the sociopath.
- Letting moments of joy, no matter how small, into our lives. Joy expands, so the more we can let in, the

more it will grow and the better we will feel.

Believe in yourself. You can do this. You can get past the experience. You may have lost your innocence, but in the end, you'll gain invaluable wisdom.

8 steps to recovery from the betrayal of a sociopath

Lovefraud received the following email from a reader; we'll call her Lisa. In one short paragraph, Lisa conveyed the betrayal, rage, pain and hopelessness that we've all felt:

> If a stranger broke into my house and stole all my valuables and then burned the rest, if I were left homeless and broke, I would be angry. I would be damaged. But I would recover. The person who did this slept in my bed and held me tight and told me he loved me every day. He told me that we were moving overseas and that everything should go. Stop paying the mortgage. Sell your furniture for cheap. Burn the rest. I did it. He disappeared with my jewelry and cash. I feel that I cannot recover. I am devastated. I am bitter. I am obsessed with my hatred and can't smile or laugh. I need a psychiatrist. I dream of stabbing him. I am a loving and forgiving person that can't find grace. I try to forgive and recognize my own fault. I fail. I need help with this.

Had an unknown criminal ransacked Lisa's home, she would be justifiably outraged, and perhaps afraid for her safety. But the man who plotted and schemed to crush her was a man that she trusted, a lover who talked about their exciting future together in a faraway land.

It was cruelty beyond belief. It was the shattering of trust.

A few months back I wrote about a book called *Legal Abuse Syndrome*. The author, Karin Huffer, writes, "The most profound loss is loss of trust."

That is what makes these experiences so painful. We trusted someone with our hopes, our dreams, our love. That person probably spoke eloquently about trust to us, in words full of shining promise. And it was all a lie.

Now we don't know whom we can trust. And we're pretty sure that we cannot trust ourselves.

So how do we recover?

8 steps for recovery

Huffer provides an outline for recovery in her book. Although the steps are geared to helping people recover from the outrages of the legal system, which has a tendency to make our bad situations even worse, I think the steps are useful for anyone recovering from the betrayal of a sociopath.

1. Debriefing. That means telling someone what happened, and that person listening without judgment. This is what we try to do at Lovefraud. We all listen to your stories, and we know what you're talking about, because we've all been there.

2. Grieving. Grief is usually associated with the death of a loved one. But as Huffer points out, it is legitimate to grieve the loss of possessions, or our lifestyle, or our place in the community. Sometimes well-meaning friends or relatives say, "Oh, it's only money." This isn't true. As Huffer writes, "Possessions are the outward manifestations of our inner identity." We didn't just lose things. We lost part of ourselves.

3. Obsession. Lisa is obsessed with her hatred of the guy who violated her. Her feelings are certainly justified. The problem with obsession, however, is that it wears you out, and interferes with your ability to regain control in your life. Huffer suggests coping with obsession by compartmentalizing it—only allowing yourself to dwell in it for specific periods of time. "Schedule your way out of it," she says.

4. Blaming. This means putting blame where it belongs: on the perpetrator. We often feel guilty for allowing the situation to occur in our lives. But we have nothing to be guilty about. We were normal, caring, loving individuals who were deceived. The guilt, anger and rage needs to directed towards the person who deceived us.

5. Deshaming. Before our encounter with the predator, we had certain beliefs, such as, "there's good in everyone," or "if someone asks me to marry him, he must really love me." Unfortunately, the dreadful experience has taught us that some beliefs are false and need to be changed. When we do this, we also change our attitude, from "I was a fool" to "I've been wronged."

6. Reframing. The first five steps of the process must be accomplished, Huffer writes, before a person can move on to reframing. At this stage, you can look at your experience, define it differently, and then articulate the wisdom you've gained.

7. Empowerment. At this point, you feel focused energy. You take ownership of your problems, determine how you are going to cope with them, and go into action.

8. Recovery. With recovery, you are able to move forward in your life. Sometimes recovery involves forgiveness, but Huffer says it is not necessary. It if far too early for Lisa, who wrote the email quoted above, to attempt forgiveness.

The long journey

There is no expected timetable for moving through the recovery process. We all have different personal histories and face different circumstances. We've all had different levels of violation.

Anyone who has been targeted for destruction by a sociopath must understand that it was a profound assault, and it will take time to recover. You may slide back and forth among the stages. So be gentle on yourself, because the journey may be long. If you keep going, in the end you will find peace, built upon new depths of wisdom and understanding.

How to attract a new relationship after the sociopath

Lovefraud received the following email from a reader who is divorced from a sociopath:

> I have a question for you. I've been divorced for 3 years now from my ex-husband who had a porn addiction. I've tried the Internet dating sites on and off since, and have had nothing but bad experiences. What do you suggest I do/ how do I go about finding someone? I am really lonely and would like to have a man in my life. However, I'm so afraid of attracting the wrong kind still. If you have any suggestions, I'd be happy to hear them.

If you've had a run-in with a sociopath, before attempting to date again, you must first heal yourself. If you're feeling lonely and afraid, it is an indication that you are not yet healed.

I believe that circumstances and situations come into our lives as a result of our internal states. The energy and emotions that we have within us are like giant magnets, bringing us more of the same. Perhaps you've heard this concept described as "The Law of Attraction." I think it's a real phenomenon, because I've seen it operate in my own life, whether I liked the results or not.

Negative emotion

When sociopaths come into our lives, they bring emotional betrayal, physical assault, financial ruin, psychological manipulation, family devastation — far more trauma than any of us ever bargained for. As a result, we are crushed, afraid, angry, frightened. Often our lives are on the verge of collapse.

We are overwhelmed by negative emotion and energy, which is totally understandable. So what happens? We get more of the same.

It happened in my life, and I've seen it in countless Lovefraud stories. The sociopath cheats on us, and we're in a car crash. The sociopath takes all our money, and then we lose our jobs. The sociopath ruins our marriage, and then we get cancer or some other major illness.

So what are we to do?

Feel the pain

I believe that we must get the negative emotion and energy out of our systems. And the way to do this is to allow ourselves to feel the pain.

Usually, this means crying. Of course, we've all probably spent hours and hours crying, and we're tired of it. We just want to stop. But the pain caused by the sociopath goes very deep, especially if we've had the predator in our lives for many years — years that we stuffed our emotions, afraid to let ourselves feel what we were really feeling. It may take a long time to release the pent-up tears.

Then there's the anger. Anger is a physical sensation — just because we know why we're angry doesn't make it go away. Anger needs to be released appropriately. (It does no good to confront the sociopath, and it may make matters worse.) My method of choice for releasing anger is visualizing the sociopath's face on a pillow, and then pounding the crap out of it. The idea is to do something physical — stomping the floor, twisting towels—until we feel an emotional release.

But what often happens as we work on releasing the pain caused by the sociopath is that we find more pain beneath it. This may be disappointment in previous love relationships, anger at mistreatment during our childhoods, betrayal bonds with other people who abused us.

These are the negative emotions that attracted the sociopath in the first place.

In my case, I was lonely, even desperate, when the sociopath showed up on my doorstep. During all of my 20s and 30s, I couldn't get a relationship with a man to work. I now know that it was due to my internal state, as described above. But when I turned 40, feeling that biological clock ticking, wanting to make a connection — well, I was primed to be plucked. Attracted by my negative internal energy, the sociopath swooped in.

With the devastation wrought by the sociopath, my pain moved to the focus of my awareness. I processed it. It was all I could do.

This is not pretty, so it is best done alone (unless you've got a really good therapist who can be with you through it). And it will take repeated sessions. You'll release some, and more will bubble to the surface. Just keep releasing, until you drain the well of pain.

Healthy and peaceful

Then an amazing thing happens — when you purge the negative energy, it is replaced by peace, hope and self-love.

I am here to tell you that it works. Changing my internal state, moving from desperate to peaceful, made all the difference in the world. Not long after I began feeling better, I met the man who became my husband — in a bar.

Some people say you can't meet anyone worthwhile in a bar, but location is not the issue. The issue is your internal state. If you're feeling positive, healthy and peaceful, an appropriate person will just show up.

My husband and I have been together since 2001. We are happy. Our relationship is comfortable and easy. There are no games, only love. And our love is not a lie — it's the real thing.

7 reasons not to seek closure from a sociopath

Relationships with sociopaths are intense. In fact, they are intentionally intense — the sociopath demands your attention, showers you with affection, and proclaims everlasting love quickly.

What's the rush? They want to hook you before you escape. All their moves are intentional.

You, of course, don't know this. You believe that the sociopaths are in hot pursuit because they are smitten and can't live without you. The two of you are, as they swear, soul mates.

Then, either suddenly or slowly, the relationship is over.

Huh? What happened? How could this person who painted a glistening picture of your future together just turn and walk away without looking back?

You want to understand what when wrong. You want closure.

If the key symptoms of a sociopath accurately describe your partner, don't bother going after closure. Here's why:

1. The intensity you saw wasn't love — it was pursuit of a prize

When sociopaths want something, they hyperfocus — they focus intently on what interests them. When your relationship started, that was you. You were the prize. Once the sociopath won you — well, there was nothing to pursue anymore.

2. Sociopaths will never feel your pain

You were in love. Now that the relationship is over, you are heartbroken. Despite what the sociopaths said, they were never in love. Why? Because they are incapable of love. They literally do not feel the pull of love the way you do. So they will never be heartbroken, and cannot share your pain.

3. Sociopaths don't care how you feel

Sociopaths do not feel empathy. They will certainly take advantage of your empathy, but they do not experience it. In fact, they view empathy as a weakness, as a stupid emotion that makes you vulnerable. And from their point of view, the only thing to do with vulnerability is to take advantage of it.

4. Sociopaths do not feel remorse

Sociopaths do not experience regret. They never feel sorry for anything they've done. Oh, they may be sorry when they're busted, but they don't regret their actions, only that they got caught.

5. Sociopaths will never apologize

You may want the sociopaths to apologize for all the pain they caused you. But a true apology requires the offenders to recognize the pain they caused — impossible for a sociopath (see above). Now, sociopaths may indeed say the words, "I'm sorry," but this is just a tactic to continue manipulating you. Don't fall for it.

6. Sociopaths feed on your emotional responses

Sociopaths love being a puppet master, pulling strings and watching other people dance. They especially like getting people to cry, plead or explode — the more visceral your response, the more satisfaction they derive from it. Don't feed the beast.

7. Seeking closure gives sociopaths an opportunity to hoover you

You may know that the relationship is bad for you, but still have difficulty staying away. Many people have met with or talked to a sociopath to end it — only to find themself "hoovered," or sucked back in, like a vacuum cleaner.

No Contact is the way forward. Seeking closure keeps you engaged with the sociopath — and it's useless. They will never understand how they've hurt you. They'll never apologize.

So don't wait for the sociopath to end it — you end it. You decide that you will no longer subject yourself to the insensitivity, disrespect, cheating, abuse — whatever the sociopath is doing. Make the decision that it's over, and stick with it.

The best way to achieve closure is to give it to yourself.

After the sociopath, learning to trust again

A Lovefraud reader posted the following comment about trust awhile back:

> I just have one question for everyone here. Does anyone trust people after these sick people did what they did to us? Unfortunately for me I have run across a few of these sickos but NONE like my ex. Whoever I meet now I'm thinking to myself, who is this person really? Do they have a secret life like the Scott Petersons and Ted Bundys of this world? I don't let my children out of my sight and I'm already training my kids and they all know the signs of a sociopath — especially my girls. I feel like I'm in a prison sometimes in my mind as I try so hard but just can't trust anyone.

Yes, it is possible to trust again. Remember, antisocials account for 1% to 4% of the population, depending on how the personality disorder is defined. Let's bump the number of disordered people up to 12% to include other exploitative manipulators, like narcissists and borderlines.

That still means that 88% of the population are not sociopaths, and may be deserving of our trust.

So how can we feel trust again? How do we determine whom to trust? I think there are four components to being able to feel trust, and deciding who deserves to be trusted.

1. Educate ourselves

One of the statements I've heard over and over again, through emails and phone calls from victims, is this: "I didn't know such evil existed." Well, now we know.

We've all learned, mostly the hard way, about sociopaths. Now that we know they exist, we need to educate ourselves about the warning signs, the patterns of behavior that may indicate someone is disordered. Lies, irresponsibility, vague answers to questions, no long-term friends, new in town, magnetic charm, lavish flattery, statements that don't add up, flashes of violence — if we start seeing the signs, we need to put up our guard.

2. Believe our own instincts

Just about everyone who was victimized by a sociopath had early warning signs — a gut feeling that something wasn't right, an instinctive revulsion, questions about what was seen or heard. Unfortunately, we ignored the signals.

We didn't believe the signals for three reasons:

1. We didn't have the empirical knowledge that evil exists (see above), so we didn't know how interpret them.
2. We viewed ourselves as open-minded individuals, and believed that everyone deserves the benefit of the doubt.
3. We allowed the sociopath to explain away our questions and doubts.

Never again. We should never doubt our instincts. In fact, we should train ourselves to pay attention to our instincts. Our intuition is absolutely the best tool we have for steering clear of sociopaths.

3. Make people earn our trust

I had a blind spot. I am a forthright, trustworthy person. I would never think of lying to someone. Unfortunately, I thought everyone else was like me. Big mistake. My younger brother's life philosophy is probably more useful. His rule of thumb: "Everyone is an a**hole until proven otherwise."

The point is that we should not give our trust away indiscriminately. People must earn our trust by consistent, reliable and truthful behavior.

Important caveat: Sociopaths often appear to be trustworthy, dependable and honest in the beginning, while they're trying to hook us. So if the good behavior slips, and bad behavior starts to appear, we must recognize the change as a big red flag.

4. Process our pain

I think the biggest roadblock to being able to trust again is our own pain. After an encounter with a sociopath, we've been deceived, betrayed, injured, emotionally crushed. We are angry and bitter, and rightfully so. But if we want to move on, we can't keep carrying the pain around.

To get rid of the pain, we must allow ourselves to feel it.

I recommend that, either privately or with the guidance of a good therapist, we let the tears and curses flow. Expressing the pain physically, without hurting yourself or others, also helps. My favorite technique was pounding pillows with my fists. You may want to stomp your feet, twist towels or chop wood.

Trust and love

It is important to be able to trust again. Doubting and disbelieving everyone we meet is a dismal way to live. If we cannot recover our trust in humanity, the sociopath who plagued us will have truly won.

The difference is that after the sociopath, we must practice informed trust. We know the red flags of a sociopath, and in evaluating a person, we make sure that we don't see them. Our intuition gives us the green light. The person has proven, and continues to prove, to be trustworthy. These are the intellectual aspects of trust.

By doing the work of exorcising our pain, we clear away the roadblocks to feeling trust emotionally. It's crucial to be able to feel trust, because that's what paves the way for love.

With the sociopath — is it love or addiction?

Editor's Note: Lovefraud received the following email from a reader whom we'll call "Gianna."

After extensive searches for the article already written, I've come to think I should just ask the question.

Will I ever be able to love someone the way I loved the sociopath?

I am 3 years out of my relationship with the man who almost destroyed me. It's taken therapy, countless books, overcoming obsession, and rebuilding myself from the ground up. I've come a long way but there is still one piece of me that is missing: My ability to love as strongly as I did before, to feel that overwhelming warmth and elation I once had when I fell in love.

I'm in a new relationship with a wonderful man. But he's not superman.

As much as I know the person I used to be in the relationship with was a fallacy, I loved him like no other. The sociopath made me high as a kite on love... in the beginning. He made me perfect. He was so cool! I had so much pride in my identity as, "his girlfriend." Then everything went wrong, years were lost in the haze of this maze. I see now what happened and what it really was but I can't forget those wonderful first feelings. I'm sad that I may never have them again. I'm resentful of that memory and wonder if I popped my cork on love.

Don't get me wrong, I love my boyfriend. He's my best friend. He's genuine, full of integrity, and I respect him. When we have miscommunications we talk about them in a healthy way. We are always seeking to understand the other's point of view. He's loving and affectionate and even good looking! I trust him completely. He's human.

So what's wrong with me? Why am I always comparing him to the impossibly perfect man from the past? A man I want nothing to do with! Why can't I love him as completely as I loved a myth? Why can't my healthy partner measure up to the wolf in sheep's clothing? Did that situation kill something inside me that I will never get back? A feeling I want so much with the man I'm with now.

If you have any advice, I'd appreciate it. I don't want the great love of my life to have been a fraud.

Donna Andersen responds

Gianna,

I'm glad you've escaped the sociopath, glad you've recovered, and glad you've found a real, authentic love.

Other people have asked similar questions: Will I ever love again? Will I ever feel the same love that I felt with sociopath?

Here's what I think is the question that really needs to be asked: Was it really love that you felt for the sociopath — or was it addiction?

The romantic love addiction

Let's start by stating this: All romantic love is addictive.

Helen Fisher, a researcher who specializes in the biology of romantic love, says that romantic love involves three distinct brain systems. These brain systems evolved over millennia to make us want to stay with one partner, so that we could raise children together, so that the human race could survive. The brain systems are activated when we fall in love, and when we lose love.

Fisher published a study in 2010 that investigated what happens to the brain after a breakup. Her team conducted an experiment with students who had recently broken up with a partner, but were still in love. The subjects looked at photos of their former partners while the researchers studied images of their brains.

According to LiveScience.com, "The researchers found that, for heartbroken men and women, looking at photographs of former partners activated regions in the brain associated with rewards, addiction cravings, control of emotions, feelings of attachment and physical pain and distress."

Furthermore, Fisher and her colleagues found that with unrequited love, these brain systems go into overdrive. In a TED talk, she explained:

> When you've been dumped, the one thing you love to do is just forget about this human being, and then go on with your life — but no, you just love them harder. As the poet Terence, the Roman poet once said, he said, "The less my hope, the hotter my love." And indeed, we now know why. Two thousand years later, we can explain this in the brain. That brain system — the reward system for wanting, for motivation, for craving, for focus — becomes more active when you can't get what you want. In this case, life's greatest prize: an appropriate mate.

So that's the background. We are biologically programmed to feel profound desire and craving for our beloved, and this desire and craving gets even more intense when we lose our beloved.

Seduced by a sociopath

Now, let's look at what happens when our beloved is, in reality, a sociopath.

Think about the sociopathic seduction. In the beginning of the relationship, this individual:

- Love bombed you — showered you with attention and affection.
- Mirrored you — seemed to share all of your interests and values.

- Seemed perfect for you — that's because he or she figured out what you were looking for and became that person.
- Rushed the relationship — quickly proclaimed his or her love and started planning a future together.
- Promised to make your dreams come true — you would live happily ever after.

Plus, most Lovefraud readers experienced all of this very quickly as an intense, whirlwind romance. This is the beginning of the psychopathic love bond.

Although I don't know of any research to back this up, I suspect that all of those desires and cravings — that are natural in any romantic relationship — are even more intense with the psychopathic love bond.

The trauma bond

Then what happened in your relationship? The sociopath did something to create fear and anxiety in the relationship. He or she disappeared with no explanation, or took your money, or suddenly raged at you, or you caught the individual lying.

Whatever. Your sweet, adoring love interest disappeared, and you wanted that person, and your storybook romance, back.

So you tried to talk it out. You wanted to solve the problem. You may have even apologized for something you didn't do, just to reclaim your special lover. Eventually the two of you kissed and made up.

But the fear of losing your love, and then the relief of regaining your love, had the effect of intensifying the psychopathic love bond that you felt even more.

When you're involved with a sociopath, this cycle tends to repeat itself — intense love and attraction, followed by intense fear and anxiety, followed by reconciliation. But with each turn of the wheel, the psychopathic love bond gets stronger and stronger.

Eventually it turns into a trauma bond.

So here is my question to Gianna, and all who have loved the sociopath with more intensity than anyone else: Are you sure it was love? Or was it an addiction that morphed into a trauma bond?

Real love after the sociopath

Here's what I know to be true: Real love, authentic love, satisfying love, is possible after the sociopath.

When I divorced the sociopath, the court awarded me all the money that he took from me, plus $1 million in punitive damages.

I spent about a year trying to collect my judgment. Eventually, I had to accept failure — I was not going to get my money back from him.

A week after I came to terms with that — believe me, it was painful — I met the man who would become my husband, Terry Kelly.

We've been together since 2001, as a married couple since 2005. And I can honestly say I love Terry far more than I ever loved James Montgomery.

And the best part is, this love is real.

7 surprising reasons why loving a cheater is actually a gift

Your partner is a heartless, unrepentant cheater. Here's why it could be good for you.

My ex-husband cheated as a way of life.

He carried on affairs with at least six women (that I know of) during our relationship — which was amazing, considering we were only together for two and a half years.

He had a child with one of those women. And then, 10 days after I left him — not after we divorced, after I left him — he married the mother of the child. It was the second time he committed bigamy.

Sorting through the file boxes full of papers he left behind — the guy was a packrat — I discovered evidence that during the seven or so years before I met him, he'd been involved with 25 or 30 women. He was married almost the entire time.

Estimates of the percentage of married men who cheat on their wives range from 25 percent to 75 percent, according to the Washington Post. Marriage Counselor M. Gary Neuman says 48 percent of men cheat because they are emotionally dissatisfied, and 66 percent of men feel guilty about it, according to WebMD.com.

My ex-husband wasn't one of those men who felt guilty about looking outside of his marriage for love. No, my ex-husband was a manipulator and an exploiter — in other words, a sociopath.

Because of my experience, I founded Lovefraud.com, to teach

people how to recognize and recover from sociopaths. After col-
lecting more than 5,000 cases, conducting three Internet surveys
and writing three books, I can tell you this—often, buried in these
relationships from hell, there's an extraordinary gift.

Here are seven reasons why you can actually benefit from loving a sociopathic cheater:

1. Take off your rose-colored glasses — there really are bad people in the world.

All our lives, we hear cultural messages that "we're all created
equal" and "everybody has good inside." This is true for most people, but not all. Millions of sociopaths live among us, and they pursue romantic relationships not for love, but for exploitation.

2. Why did you fall for him? Take stock of your own vulnerabilities.

Sociopaths hook you by targeting your vulnerabilities. If
you're human, you have vulnerabilities. This doesn't mean you're
weak — anything you desire, such as love or a family, can make
you vulnerable. You need to know what your buttons are, so you
can recognize if someone is pushing them.

3. The pain of sociopathic betrayal is so intense that you must cry.

You, like many people, may have dealt with heartache by picking yourself up and moving on. You locked your heartache away
in an internal closet — where it festered. But when you've been involved with a sociopath, you are so hurt, and they are so cold-
hearted, that you cannot hold back the tears — and this is the first
step towards healing.

4. You have an opportunity to process the pain of previous betrayals.

Perhaps a prior husband or boyfriend also cheated on you.
Perhaps you were abused as a child — and you never dealt with
the trauma. You may discover that this new betrayal feels exactly
like what you endured before. Let the tears flow for all the pain —

and you'll be well on your way to recovery.

5. You become less judgmental of others.

If you were involved with a sociopathic cheater, you were deceived and manipulated. But still, you fell for it. In the past, you may have wondered how people got themselves into such insane situations. Now you know that it can happen to anyone.

6. You learn to listen to your intuition.

Most people betrayed by a sociopathic cheater have a gut feeling, or intuition, early on, that there is something wrong with the person or the relationship. Most people ignore it. Your intuition will almost always warn you when someone is dangerous. After this painful experience, commit to listening to your instincts.

7. Real healing will lead to a real relationship, with someone who truly loves you.

It will take time to recover from profound betrayal. But if you give yourself permission to heal, and commit yourself to doing the internal work required, you can come out of this experience healthier than ever, and ready for a truly rewarding relationship.

I can tell you from personal experience, a relationship with a sociopathic cheater is devastating. But I had two choices — fall completely apart, or work to recover.

I chose recovery, and it was worth it. I am now happily married to a wonderful man, and my relationship is everything I ever wanted.

After the sociopath, I still feel numb — what can I do?

Lovefraud received the following email from a heartbroken reader:

> It has been about 3 years since I discovered what happened to me. I've had no contact with my spaths. Yet I still feel so numb and broken. I feel like I have tried almost everything to get through this dark time. I feel so lost. I feel so robbed of my life and my children have been too. What can I do now? I'm running out of solutions. I don't want to feel like this anymore.... please suggest something for me.

Many, many Lovefraud readers have had this experience. I know I did.

Overwhelmed

When you first realize the magnitude of your betrayal by a sociopath, you are overwhelmed. At the very least, the sociopath has deceived and manipulated you. This individual may have also stolen from you, assaulted you, smeared your name and perhaps even tried to kill you.

From the time you discovered what was really going on, each day might have brought shocking new revelations about his or her behavior.

So in addition to coming to grips with what this individual did to you, you likely experienced another major shock to your system. This is it: Evil really does exist.

You may not have believed it before. You may have bought into the cultural myth of "Everybody has good inside." Now, because of your own experience, you have to admit that some people are rotten to the core. This may totally upend your view of the world.

In short, the impact of a sociopath crashing into your life is so shocking and devastating that you cannot absorb it all. So, as a protective measure, you block your feelings about what has happened. You go numb.

Opening the box

Feeling numb blocks the pain — but it also blocks joy and happiness. So although going to numbness is appropriate for a while, it's not a good place to spend the rest of your life.

So how do you escape feeling numb?

You begin to allow yourself to feel the emotion attached to your experience.

Most likely, you packed all the pain, anger and grief over the sociopath's exploitation into an tight emotional box that you shoved into a closet deep within you, vowing never to open it.

The only way to get back to your feeling self is to open that box.

It's okay that you weren't able to do it previously. When you first learned the truth, you likely needed to deal with all the practical matters associated with sociopathic destruction, such as stabilizing your finances, work, children or housing. Facing these issues could have demanded all of the psychological, emotional and physical energy that you had.

Internal recovery

But perhaps the practical life issues are reasonably stable, and you can now turn to your internal recovery.

You may have been afraid to do it. You may have felt like if you allowed yourself to feel that deep pain, you would start crying and never stop.

But I suggest that you find the courage to open the box. Allow yourself to feel the pain, because by feeling it, you release it.

This will not be pretty. You may find yourself crying uncontrollably, wailing, pounding your fists, collapsing. I recommend that you do this in private, or perhaps with the help of a competent, understanding therapist.

It also will not be fast. You most likely have layers and layers of pain. Some will rise to the top, you will purge, you will feel some relief, and then more pain will rise up. The process will take time.

But releasing the pain enables the emotional wounds to heal. And the healing will restore your sense of vitality and aliveness.

Emotional recovery can be a difficult path to walk. But each step you take is a step towards wholeness and happiness — which is much more fulfilling than a life of numbness.

After 6 months of No Contact,
the sociopath wants to begin again

Months ago, I received email from a Lovefraud reader whom we'll call, "Alana." Here is the exchange:

Alana wrote:

> Donna, I came across ur website accidentally after I left a guy and was searching for some answers on whether he was abusive, I was left totally confused.
>
> When I met him 4 years ago, he seemed so crazy about me and he would send me hundreds of texts per day and 10 phone calls, he wanted to see me every day. At first I felt suffocated I wanted to run in the other direction, but he kept telling me I'm the best thing ever and his words are so poetic, I thought wow, it's so different cause this guy really is obsessed with me, he's so different from the rest of them who want to play the field and take their time or never call back. My best friend said oh my god he's obsessed with u, and he talks like this to u?! Ur never going to be able to leave.
>
> But then he has an ugly side to him. He loses his temper on me, pressures me for sex, he was rigid about everything. He was also a control freak, over the years he broke up with me for going to the gym, having lunch with female friends, putting other things above him. I still thought it was all because he just cared about me so much, but then

I found out he does whatever he likes and doesn't tell me about. He punishes me for things he's done himself. I got quite resentful.

I tried to leave him so many times. But I always end up going back to him cause he would chase me. He said I abandoned him every time I left; he's threatened to kill himself several times. He also threatened to show my pictures to everyone else if I abandon him. After all these things failed, he started going to church, he became Mr. Wonderful overnight. I seriously don't know what happened, but he seems to have changed, and he says he loves me and wants to make it up to me.

He still makes me cry, and he's so indifferent because when I cry, he doesn't stop yelling and he puts me on speaker and goes silent when I'm sobbing. Sometimes I feel he has no emotions unless they are his. He often smiles when I catch him in a lie too. It creeps me out totally.

We finally took a break. He actually honored his words and gave me a month to think. I didn't want to go back after a month so I never contacted him again. Then he started writing me again, he told me how thankful he is to ever known me and I will always be number one in his heart, but for now space is best, and that he is really doing ok thanks to all I've taught him, and how I've made him such a good person.

Donna, what am I dealing with here? I'm so confused. I don't want to judge him, but I've been so hurt — idk who I'm dealing with anymore. Is it the guy who truly loves me or is it someone totally sick and manipulative?

I replied:

The guy is a sociopath. He is incapable of love, so I'm afraid he never loved you. It is all about control. He wants to control you.

Do not go back to him. In fact, do not have any contact with him at all. In order for you to recover, you need to stay away from him. They are experts at reeling you back in if you give him the slightest opening.

The other day, I received another email from Alana:

> Hi Donna, as u can see I wrote u six months ago. Since then, I've cut off all contact. I blocked phone numbers through my phone company, I blocked every email address. I changed routines and routes, I quit one of my jobs so I'd never run into him. I don't use social media, and I made myself to quit googling his. I've never looked.
> I've kept no contact firm and steady for six months. And then, he wrote me from a newly created email address. He begged for my return, he said if I don't respond then he'd be damaged forever by what I'm doing to him.
> Of course I felt an enormous amount of guilt. I wrote back out of guilt and shame. But I said I don't hate u, I just want to heal and I asked him to just leave it like this. He didn't write me back. I have that sick feeling again. I hate myself for writing back out of sympathy.
> I am still keeping no contact and moving past this set back. It's the right choice, right?

I replied:

> Yes. Please recognize that his "damaged forever" plea is just manipulation. His intention is to reel you in again. If you return, you will experience all of the atrocious behavior all over again. Commit to yourself again to No Contact. Do not respond, no matter what he says.

Do they return?

People often ask me, do sociopaths return? As this story illustrates, sometimes, unfortunately, they do.

In Alana's case, the guy waited six months. I've heard of other cases in which the sociopath has been gone for years, and has turned up again.

Why? Why, when they seem to have finally gotten the message and disappeared, do they all of a sudden pop up?

The answer is simple. They were able to manipulate you before, so they'll try to manipulate you again.

Sometimes the sociopaths are desperate — perhaps their newest target has caught on to the scam, and has thrown them out. They need to find new supply, and fast.

Other times, the sociopaths are just trolling. They're putting the hooks out to see if you will bite.

Sixth sense

Quite a few people have told me that just when they finally felt they were getting over the experience with a sociopath, just when they were starting to finally relax – that's when the sociopath initiated contact.

Sociopaths often seem to have a sixth sense about when you might be receptive to hearing from them.

In fact, some people actually felt they had recovered enough, and were strong enough, to be "friends" with the sociopath.

It didn't work. Although the sociopaths stayed on good behavior for a while, sooner or later the lying, manipulation and abuse began again. The targets felt all the old pain and betrayal. Except this time it was worse, because the targets were also angry at themselves for opening the door and letting the sociopaths in.

And, their recovery was back at square one.

No Contact is forever

If you've been involved with a sociopath, once you get the person out of your life, make sure he or she stays out.

This may feel uncomfortable. You know how you would feel if someone turned their back on you, so you don't want to do it to another person, even a sociopath.

Remember, sociopaths do not feel the way that you feel.

Alana wrote back out of "guilt and shame." But I assure you, the sociopath did not experience any guilt or shame, no matter how badly he treated her. He knew that Alana is a nice woman, and tried to use that to his advantage with his claim that he would be "damaged forever."

Yeah, right. Had Alana let him proceed, he would soon be back to his old controlling ways. Even though she temporarily relapsed, I'm so glad Alana quickly recovered and went back to No Contact.

To protect yourself forever, remember this: No Contact is forever.

10 reasons why sociopaths really are losers

If you're struggling to get over an encounter with a sociopath — whether a romantic relationship or some other involvement — keep this in mind: They are losers.

They are not worth any emotional energy that you are spending on them, or any pain that you feel. Here are 10 reasons why:

1. Sociopaths cannot love the way you do

The root of serious personality disorders — antisocial, narcissistic, borderline, histrionic and psychopathy — is an impaired ability to love. These people cannot feel empathy like you do. They are not interested in caregiving — a critical component of real love. People diagnosed as antisocials or psychopaths are not capable of love at all.

2. Sociopaths cannot be trusted

What do antisocials and psychopaths really want in life? Power and control. Their objective is always to win — whatever that may look like at the moment. So they always have an ulterior motive, and for that reason, can never be trusted.

3. Sociopaths are empty inside

They have no real passion. Oh, they may have temporary obsessions, but they do not care deeply about any person, thing, place or ideal. Without any real depth, they are caricatures of human beings, cardboard cut-outs, creatures without substance.

4. Sociopaths have no real friends

They have minions. They have co-conspirators. They have dupes. But because of items 1, 2 and 3 above, sociopaths do not have friends. They really are alone in the world. It's sad.

5. Sociopaths have no real family

Yes, they have parents, spouses, children and relatives (possibly including you), but no one involved will feel a sense of family. The sociopath will just take advantage of relatives, and any relatives who are not themselves disordered will feel abused.

6. Sociopaths' schemes fall apart

They're always coming up with get-rich-quick schemes, grandiose plans that depend on other people's money. Sometimes the plans never get off the ground. Sometimes they get started, and then sputter to a halt. Sooner or later, sociopathic schemes usually fail.

7. Sociopaths have financial problems

Even when they have a job or profession, they often have financial problems. They get fired. They lose contracts. They get sued. But often when there's a money crisis, other people pay, not them.

8. Sociopaths have legal problems

Many sociopaths are criminals. In fact, the definitions of antisocial personality disorder and psychopathy refer to criminal behavior. But even those who aren't arrested for crimes are frequently involved lawsuits, divorces and child custody battles. None of this really bothers the sociopaths, but it will bother you.

9. Sociopaths crash and burn

Sociopaths may race along for awhile, living on the edge — maybe even for years. But at some point, their unconscionable behavior tends to catch up with them. Their financial empires collapse. They end up estranged from everyone in their lives. They may finally be arrested. Sooner or later, for many sociopaths, it all falls apart.

10. Sociopaths tend to die earlier

Promiscuous sex, drugs, crime, violence — this is how many sociopaths live. Whether it's health problems, accidents from risky behavior or angering the wrong person, many sociopaths end up dead. And those who don't may suffer a lonely old age. If anyone takes care of them, it's because of a sense of duty, although I don't think it's warranted.

If you're struggling to break the bonds you feel with a sociopath, refer to this list. Really, they are not worth the aggravation.

Moral dilemma: warning the next victim

Lovefraud received the following email from a reader whom we'll call Alfred. The subject line of his email was, "A moral obligation?"

I'm two years removed from the brutal break-up with my ex-spath and all in all, can say I'm doing quite well and have recovered nicely! It was a LONG journey to get to the place I'm at and it's a relief to be there after two years of continual obsessing and ruminating — I've finally reached the point where I just don't care anymore. The shock of what I had in my life for 14 years has finally dissipated — the last emotion to go.

That being said, I know I still have some work to do on myself as evidenced by my need to periodically check-up on my ex via social media. I like to think I do so to stay ahead of the game but there's certainly a thirst to quench my curiosity over what has become of the monster. Not only is he a textbook spath, but he's also a crystal meth addict! I did a little online research and am now pretty certain that he is dating the person he was triangulating me with towards the end of our relationship. My dilemma is, do I warn that person? There are good reasons in the yes and no columns and I just don't know what to do.

In the 'No' column:
This person/new source was possibly knowingly hav-

ing an affair with my ex with the knowledge that he was in a "monogamous" relationship so he'll eventually get what he deserves when he becomes the discarded.

My ex very likely lives a miserable life with few friends/subjects and is in a constant battle vs. his drug addiction — I have some fear about him harming himself as a result of any action I might take and I do not want to be or feel responsible for that.

No Contact has been in place for a year and a half and my stirring the pot, even if I did it anonymously, could be detrimental to me and my continued recovery, as it's likely my ex would know who was responsible.

In the 'Yes' column:

Even though I won the end game (he got $0 from me after I discovered and exposed his drug addiction to his family and close "friends") and threatened his career (he works with children!), delivering another blow to him would feel really good in many ways.

The new "source" is quite possibly the naive guy I once was who has been completely love-bombed and deceived as I was and as a good person, I have a moral obligation to try to warn him. I guess what I'm really trying to figure out is, would I be doing this for myself or the new target? Any advice for me?

Think of yourself first

Alfred,

Congratulations on getting away from the sociopath, on maintaining No Contact, and on your tremendous progress towards recovery.

Many, many people write to Lovefraud with exactly the same question: Am I morally obligated to warn the next victim? Your analysis is thoughtful, and shows awareness of your conflicting motivations.

Here's what I think: Your first obligation is to yourself.

Your primary concern is your own safety, recovery and peace of mind. If reaching out to the next victim puts you in jeopardy in any way, don't do it. If the sociopath will retaliate, if you're worried about being drawn back into the vortex, if just thinking about what to do triggers you, you probably should not get involved.

On the other hand

But there are other considerations. One of the prime reasons why sociopaths are able to continue their marauding ways is because no one talks about what they do. As a society, we don't talk about the fact that human predators live among us. On a personal level, keeping quiet about exploiters we know allows them to get away with their cruel, and sometimes criminal, behavior.

So I think that if you can warn someone safely, you should do it. If you warn, one of three things will happen:

1. The target will believe you and take your warning seriously.
2. The target will not believe you, probably because he is being love bombed, and the sociopath has already convinced him that you are the crazy, psycho ex.
3. The target will not believe you right away, but will remember your warning when the sociopath's mask slips and he starts to see the exploitative behavior.

If you are going to warn, you need to be fine with whatever happens. If the target does not believe you, you need to be able to shrug and say to yourself, "I tried."

Another possible option is to not do anything immediately, but wait to see if an opportunity arises.

Sooner or later, the new target will experience the sociopath's manipulation, deceit and possibly abuse. At that point, he may reach out to you, and be much more receptive to your message. It may be a good time to talk about your experience, as long as you can do it safely.

Moral obligation

So do we have a moral obligation to warn the next victim?

As I said, I believe our highest moral obligation is taking care of ourselves. We are all on our own journey, and our top priority is our own learning, growth and healing.

But being able to warn another person may be a step in our own growth. We may feel that the best thing for our own journey is to take a stand.

In the end, to warn or not to warn a question we must all answer for ourselves.

Hooked by a sociopath again

A week ago, a Lovefraud reader returned. She first wrote to Lovefraud in 2008, as she was scrambling to get away from a man who she thought was her true love, but turned out to be a sociopath.

She read Lovefraud articles and posted comments for a couple of years, and then moved on.

Until a week ago, when she sent me an email with the subject line, "I'm back." She'd become involved with another sociopath.

"How could I be so stupid?" she wrote. "And this time is much much much much worse than the last."

Another sociopath

Why does this happen? Why do we get rid of one problem person, only to find another one?

Before we are educated, we may run across one exploitative individual after another, but don't realize that there's a common denominator among them — that they are all sociopaths. We haven't yet learned that there is a psychological reason for their manipulative behavior.

But once we spend time on Lovefraud, we know.

We know that some men and women are simply disordered. We know that these disordered people are not going to change. We know the warning signs to look out for.

So after we know about sociopaths, why do we fall for them again?

Is it a case of, "Fool me once, shame on you. Fool me twice, shame on me?"

No, it's not.

Deeper injury

If we fall for another sociopath after we've learned that they exist, it means we have more healing to do.

The healing may be related to the previous sociopath, the one that initially led us to Lovefraud. But most likely, the healing that we now need is related to an older and deeper emotional injury.

Remember, sociopaths are able to hook us because they target our vulnerabilities. Sometimes the vulnerability is obvious, like a woman who is single, getting older, and wants to have children before it's too late. (That was me.)

But sometimes the vulnerability goes back further. We may have had disordered parents or siblings. We may have been abused by a teacher, clergyman or family friend, but were afraid to remember it.

Sometimes we weren't mistreated at all. But we had deep-seated beliefs that we were unwanted or unlovable — beliefs that made us a target.

Whatever our vulnerabilities, sociopaths sense them, like sharks sense blood in the water.

Ready to heal

Believe it or not, another encounter with a sociopath may be a good sign a sign that we are finally ready to work on the really deep wounds within us.

The first sociopath may have drawn our attention to the emotional injuries that were fairly close to the surface of our awareness. We cried, we kicked and screamed, we released the negative emotion of the relationship.

But when we encounter another sociopath, one "much much much much worse," and begin to process the pain of the experience, we may see that it is directly connected to a deeper injury.

When the deeper injury occurred, we may not have had the awareness or strength to deal with it. So we swept it under the carpet, walled it off in a corner of our being, and did our best to move on.

But now we do have the strength.

Embrace the healing

So Life brings us another sociopath. Why? To help us excavate all of the remaining pain, from this relationship and every negative experience that came before it.

Embrace the healing. Focus on letting go of any internal injuries that you've tried to ignore.

When you make a complete recovery, you'll be able to spot any future sociopaths right away and prevent them from entering your life.

You'll also be happy, healthy, vibrant and totally alive. Life will respond by bringing you wonderful people and experiences.

Sociopaths, pain and the Primal Scream

The Primal Scream — I remember this book being all the rage when it was published in 1970, even though at the time I had just started high school. Everyone was talking about the book, by Arthur Janov, and the therapy he developed, called primal therapy.

For me, that was the end of it. I never read the book. I never heard anything more about Arthur Janov. I haven't thought about Primal Scream or primal therapy in more than 40 years, until a few weeks ago, when a Lovefraud reader brought it up.

The reader sent me a link to an article on Arthur Janov's blog. (Yes, he's still alive — he'll soon be 90 years old.) The article was is entitled *Why we need safety,* and it was published on June 30, 2014. I invite you to read it on ArthurJanov.com.

Amoebas and tears

In the article, Janov explains how amoeba placed in water contaminated with ink will absorb the dirty water. Then, when the amoeba are placed in clean water, they discharge the black ink. They are in a place where they can purify themselves, so they do.

What is the correlation to people? Janov says people need a welcoming environment to get rid of all the pain inside. But he believes conventional therapy may not always provide it. He writes:

> That is exactly what is missing in psychotherapy. First, a notion of all the tears inside that must be experienced, and secondly, the need to provide an environment where those tears can be let out in full force.

He goes on to write,

> Psychotherapy that evades and avoids emotions makes the patient sicker. Tears must emanate from felt pain, not as an intellectual exercise, not as directed by a well-meaning counselor but tears that arrive automatically when the actual early memory is evoked.

Janov's basic premise is that early traumas felt as a fetus in the womb or as a small child get trapped in the body. Releasing the early traumas allows a person to heal.

So Janov developed "primal therapy." Here is how he explains it on his website, PrimalTherapy.com:

What is Primal Therapy?

Painful things happen to nearly all of us early in life that get imprinted in all our systems which carry the memory forward making our lives miserable. It is the cause of depression, phobias, panic and anxiety attacks and a whole host of symptoms that add to the misery. We have found a way into those early emotional archives and have learned to have access to those memories, to dredge them up from the unconscious, allowing us to re-experience them in the present, integrate them and no longer be driven by the unconscious.

Pain to vulnerability

Plenty of people don't like Arthur Janov's primal therapy. In fact, according to Wikipedia, primal therapy is listed in one book called *Crazy Therapies* and another book called *Insane Therapy*.

But I do think there is validity to Janov's key point: Emotional pain from prior experiences can get stuck within us, causing us psychological and emotional problems, and even physical illness.

In addition to this, I also believe emotional pain from prior experiences makes us susceptible to sociopaths.

This can happen in a multitude of ways. Perhaps our parents were abusive, neglectful, or simply too busy to provide us with the attention and love that we needed. Perhaps we were abused or humiliated by siblings or other family members. Perhaps we were betrayed by romantic partners that we encountered before the sociopath.

All of these situations create vulnerabilities. Sociopaths sense vulnerabilities. They identify our vulnerabilities and use them to hook us. You all know what happens after that.

Deep healing

The pain we experience because of sociopaths — betrayal, disappointment, grief — is profound. It sears us to the center of our souls.

Then it stays there — creating emotional havoc until we get the pain out of our system.

Here's where I agree with some of Janov's ideas. I believe that in order to really purge the pain that's deep within us, we need to let it rip — crying, wailing, stomping our feet.

Now, this is not pretty, and it's unlikely that you'll be able to do it in front of your friends or family, because they will want you to stop. In fact, many therapists may not be comfortable in this situation.

So do it alone. When you don't have to worry about holding yourself together for someone else's benefit, you can cry really hard, and that's when you experience release.

As you do this, you may suddenly feel a direct emotional connection between the pain caused by the sociopath and memories of pain from your past. This is good. This means you're accessing the root of the problem, those earlier betrayals and disappointments that were still stuck within you.

So is this Janov's primal scream? I don't know. But I believe that by releasing all the pain, even the early pain, you'll open yourself up for a really deep and profound healing. I know I did.

Recovering from a sociopath by living your life

You're in meltdown. You've come to the conclusion that you've been involved with a sociopath, and that everything this person told you was a lie, from the details of his or her life to the proclamations of undying love.

Now it all makes sense. Now you understand how the unbelievable headiness of the whirlwind romance (love bombing) morphed into the silent treatment, unexplained absences and unprovoked rages (devalue and discard).

You have discovered the truth: The person you fell in love with never existed. Everything you saw and experienced was an act designed to exploit you.

You are crushed. Overwhelmed by disappointment and betrayal, the emotional pain is almost unbearable. So you ask, when will this go away?

How long does it take to recover?

The short answer is that it will take as long as it takes. But the important answer is that you don't have to wait until you are fully recovered before you can live your life.

In fact, living your life helps you recover.

The two-track plan

This isn't going to be like taking a course, where you attend for a specific length of time and then get your diploma.

It's also not like going to a doctor when you're physically ill. You don't take a pill for a few weeks or months and then feel better.

Recovery from the sociopath is a two-track plan. It is about emotional recovery, and rebuilding your life. The good news is that you can, and should, work on both tracks at the same time. In fact, progress on one track will help you move along the other track.

Conscious decision

Your crucial first step is consciously deciding that you're going to do what you need to in order to recover.

At first you may not want to. You may be tempted to sweep everything that happened under the rug, assuming that time heals all ills and sooner or later you'll feel better. That's possible, but it will take longer than if you do the personal work to recover.

Or, you may skip the work and think you're feeling better, until something comes along — like a new relationship — and all the buried pain rises to the surface. It may even sabotage your new chance at happiness.

Here's another reason to decide to do the work: If you don't fully recover from the pain inflicted by a sociopath, you are susceptible to falling for another sociopath. Embracing recovery can make a difference for the rest of your life.

Emotional recovery

So, back to the meltdown.

When it comes to your emotional recovery from the sociopathic betrayal, crying is good. Wailing is good. Curling up in a ball on the floor is good. Pounding a punching bag to release your anger is good. Any means of expression that naturally arises is good, as long as it is not destructive to you, other people, your pets or property.

The idea is to get the negative emotional energy out of your system.

Now, this is not pretty. Your friends and family most likely will not have the ability to be around you as you process your emotions. It is simply too distressing for other people, and they will want you to stop. But that's not your objective. Your objective is to allow yourself to cry and wail until you feel a release.

Therefore, I recommend doing the processing alone. Even if you have a therapist, you may want to save your appointments for talking about what happened and gaining insight. But keep in mind that you can't talk away your feelings. Even if you understand why you feel the way you do, you still need to process the emotions.

Drilling for oil

This process is like drilling for oil. You'll hit a pool of pain, and the black goo will rise to the surface. You do some more drilling, and you'll hit another pool, which will spout forth. The idea is to keep going until you drain all the black gooey pools of negative energy. Depending on how long you've been exposed to the sociopath, you may have many of them, so this can take awhile.

Eventually you'll discover that one of the black pools is linked to some other experience or belief from earlier in your life — one that made you vulnerable to the sociopath in the first place. Finding this is the equivalent of finding a gusher.

This is your objective — discovering and releasing the hidden pain that has skewed your perceptions and created a place within you for the sociopath to set his or her hooks. Addressing this issue — whatever it is — changes everything.

Adding joy

Draining off the pain creates voids within you, holes where the goo used to be. What do you do with them? You fill them with anything that brings you joy.

While you're in meltdown, this may seem totally bogus. How can you possibly think about joy when your life is falling off a cliff? At least, that was my reaction when I received this advice. Everything was crumbling, and I'm supposed to do something to make me happy?

Well, guess what. It works. Any small activity that brings you an internal smile will do — playing with your pets, going for a walk, enjoying a sunset. Filling those voids with little pieces of joy and happiness eventually changes your entire internal structure. Instead of pools of black gooey pain inside, you'll feel a growing sense of peace.

Living your life

The second track of recovery, as I said, is living your life. Part of this is dealing with the practical and logistical problems created by the sociopath, such as money, your job, your home or your children.

These can, of course, be really big problems, and I don't want to downplay them. The important point here is that because you're following two tracks, you don't need to solve all of these problems before beginning your emotional recovery. You work both tracks at once.

Again, as you resolve these issues, it's important to rebuild other areas of your life at the same time. Reconnect with old friends that the sociopath pushed out of your life. Go back to activities that the sociopath made difficult or impossible — art, music, gardening, watching old movies, whatever you enjoyed. Or, start new activities.

Be sure to take care of your health. Eat right, avoid drugs and excessive alcohol, and get exercise. In fact, exercise can go a long way towards relieving depression and anxiety. It's sometimes as effective as medication.

Living is recovery

Your recovery will likely seem uneven — two steps forward and one step back. But even halting progress is progress. By putting one foot in front of the other, you'll keep moving down the tracks — both of them.

Life brings opportunities. Perhaps you'll have an opportunity to make new friends, or get a new job, or move to a new community. If the opportunity feels right, be open to it. You never know where it could lead you.

Living your life the way you want to is recovery.

Getting back on track
after the ruin of a sociopath

A Lovefraud reader who posts as "LadyA" sent Lovefraud the following email.

I've spent a lot time thinking about my experience with my spath, and how it affected me and the people around me. I have read article after article, story after story. I now fully understand what spaths do and how they do it — but I didn't understand why I don't feel any better about it. What was I missing?

When I left my spath it was a fairly dramatic experience. He had just been sentenced to serve jail time on the weekends for an obstruction of justice charge. My mom flew into town and in one swoop we packed up everything we could get in the car and left the province to go back to my hometown. I had to quit my job over email and send a goodbye text to all my friends.

I am thankful every day for what my mom did for me. I sure wasn't happy about it at the time but I knew I needed out and this was my chance. What I didn't know is how much moving back to my hometown would affect me emotionally. I had originally planned on only being back for six months. Just long enough for him to move on and get me out of mind, but it has now been just over three years and I still haven't moved back. I got settled in a new job, new friends, and a new relationship. Even after all of this I haven't been able to figure out why I'm not happy. Until three days ago.

Pride. I was proud of myself for the life that I had built. I moved 1200 km's away from home right after high school to a big city. I was on the fast track to a strong career in a competitive field. I had a brand new car, paid all my bills on time, and was saving to buy a house. I was independent, reliable, strong, caring, and had a really great outlook on the world. Not many people can say that at 22.

All of that was ruined by a six-month "whirlwind romance." I'm no longer proud of myself. I feel like I have failed because I came back home with my "tail between my legs" to my mommy. I no longer have a new car because it was repossessed as soon as I got back here. I am jaded, I don't trust people easily, and I am no longer as strong as the face I put on the outside. I've gained weight because deep down I just don't care anymore. My career is now on a plateau due to the location where I live. I don't have one reason to be proud of myself right now.

How do I get my pride back when I know what happened? I want to feel proud of myself for my life but I just have zero idea where to start. I've thought about moving away again, but I don't really know if that's the answer. How can I be proud of what has happened in my life? I'm really honestly just so ashamed.

Donna Andersen responds

Dear LadyA,

I am so sorry about your encounter with a sociopath. The good news is that you can recover.

Right now, however, it does not seem that way. Why? I can see two reasons.

The first is that betrayal by a sociopath is a huge emotional injury. In the beginning of your email you said that, after all your reading, you now "fully understand what spaths do and how they do it," but you don't feel any better.

Understanding sociopaths is a critical first step to recovery. But understanding is an intellectual process, something that you do with your mind. The wound you experienced is also emotional. It needs to be dealt with emotionally.

How do you do that? You allow yourself to feel the pain of the injury.

This means letting yourself cry. Letting yourself scream and wail. Letting yourself experience anger — I'm sure there is anger — perhaps by working it out on a punching bag.

This isn't pretty, and you probably want to do it privately, because other people often have difficulty being around this. Or, you may have a good therapist who can help you.

One way or another, any bottled up emotion you have within you needs to come out.

Underestimated the injury

Next you wrote that you identified the reason that you're not happy as "pride." But it seems like you are regarding pride as something bad, like one of the seven deadly sins.

You had every reason to be proud, because your pride was based on your achievement. And the sociopath took this away from you.

Here is what I think has happened: You have underestimated the scale of the injury, and the severity of the betrayal.

LadyA, you were building a life for yourself. You went out on your own; you started building a career; you were moving forward.

And some manipulative, deceitful parasite, who did something bad enough to end up in jail, ruined it for you.

Not only did he cost you money and hurt your career, he corrupted your outlook on life. You're jaded; you don't trust; you don't care. You are not the young person you once were — all because of the sociopath.

Recognize that this was not a normal breakup — after all, you had to flee your home, job and friends.

Your life was shattered. Your psyche was deflated. This is a massive shock to your system. It's no wonder that you are still struggling.

Drain the emotion

So what do you do? In my opinion, you do exactly what I suggested earlier — allow yourself to feel the pain now, knowing that the pain is bigger than you originally thought.

So you cry. You stomp. You imagine him standing in front of you and yell at him. (Do not, however, attempt to confront him in person. This would be counterproductive.)

The idea is to drain off the negative emotion.

As you drain the emotion, a void will be created within you. It's very important to fill that void with joy.

This may sound preposterous to you, like you have no reason to be joyful. But don't look at the totality of your life right how.

Do any small thing that makes you happy: Go for a walk. Play with your pets. Have lunch with a friend. Listen to music.

Your recovery may require many rounds of draining off the negative and replacing it with positive. But with time, you'll find that your entire outlook will change, and you'll be able to get back on track.

Importantly, with the wisdom you gained through this experience, you'll never fall for a sociopath again.

True recovery from the sociopath through tapping and energy psychology

I believe true recovery from sociopathic betrayal is literally in our own hands.

Many people have quietly become aware of a healing technique known by several names: tapping, energy psychology, emotional freedom techniques (EFT). Using this approach, many people have recovered from emotional pain, physical pain, illness, anxiety, depression and PTSD.

So what is it? With your fingers, you tap certain points on your body — mostly on your face — while bringing to mind specific aspects of the condition that you want to heal. The tapping creates an electrical charge that breaks the connection between your memory of your experience and how you feel today.

It doesn't matter when the past experience happened. I've often written here on Lovefraud that sociopaths come into our lives because of a pre-existing vulnerability. We have suffered a previous hurt, betrayal or misunderstanding, and the trauma is still buried in our subconscious. Sociopaths, with their uncanny ability to discover our vulnerabilities, use them to hook us.

Tapping enables us to not only recover from our most recent betrayals, but from the long-buried injuries as well.

Books

A book called, *The Tapping Solution: A revolutionary system for stress-free living,* by Nick Ortner is now a best-seller.

I haven't yet read *The Tapping Solution,* but I read another book on the topic called *The Promise of Energy Psychology,* by David Feinstein, Donna Eden and Gary Craig. I was so thoroughly impressed by the book that I became convinced that this approach is the future of healing.

Energy psychology, Feinstein explains, is a combination of ancient Eastern techniques for shifting the energies of the body and conventional Western ideas in psychology. When you use the technique, you are tapping on special acupuncture points to change your conditioned responses. Feinstein writes:

> Stimulating energy points on the skin, paired with specified mental activities, can instantly shift your brain's electrochemistry to:
> • help overcome unwanted emotions such as fear, guilt, shame, jealousy, or anger,
> • help change unwanted habits and behavior, and
> • enhance you abilities to love, succeed, and enjoy life.

Feinstein isn't a New Age charlatan. He is trained as a clinical psychologist and spent seven years on the faculty at Johns Hopkins University. Visit his website at www.innersource.net.

One of the really difficult psychological problems that energy psychology has proven to resolve is PTSD — post-traumatic stress disorder. How does it do this? It breaks the connection between a trigger and the body's autonomic nervous system, which generates the fight, flight or freeze responses. For this reason alone, I believe any Lovefraud reader who is suffering from PTSD should investigate energy psychology.

Tapping is easy. You can do it as often as necessary, and it can't hurt you. You don't even have to believe in tapping for it to work. Once you learn the technique, you can do it yourself, which makes it free.

If you have severe psychological problems, you should probably consult with a trained practitioner.

Why tapping works

Here's what I really like about this tapping technique — it's founded in science, although not necessarily conventional science.

As part of *The Tapping Solution* video event, the author posted a half-hour video interview with Bruce Lipton, a cellular biologist and best-selling author. I actually liked this interview better than the movie, because Lipton explains, from a scientific perspective, how our mind works and how we can use our mind to heal ourselves.

This technique works

Tapping can relieve emotional and physical pain, which is huge. But it can also do more.

EFT tapping can help you achieve personal goals that require peak performance. In fact, the *Promise of Energy Psychology* book contains several examples of competitive athletes who enhanced their skills through tapping.

Tapping can help you anytime you need to be at your best, such as during a presentation. That's how I've used it.

All my life, I never thought of myself as a public speaker. But since my run-in with a sociopath, and after learning so much about the disorder, I now have something important to say. That means I've had to become comfortable with getting up in front of people and speaking, which, as you probably know, many people fear more than death.

So I used tapping to alleviate my stress about public speaking and increase my comfort level. I've also used tapping to deal with remnants of the pain about my losses due to the sociopath, which still, 13 years after my divorce, occasionally crop up.

I can say that tapping works.

Why sociopaths keep showing up

A Lovefraud reader recently sent me the following important question:

> I seem to only attract what I believe are sociopaths into my life — even when I am not trying to find anyone. I feel as if they find me and try to befriend me. Is there some kind of an explanation for this?

This reader posts as "Sam." Last year I published her story as a Letter to Lovefraud called, *I have no further use to him and I am being disposed of.*

The explanation for her current experience is in her story, which is absolutely tragic. Here is what happened to her:

- She witnessed domestic violence from a very young age.
- She left home before she turned 15.
- She suffered from depression.
- Her first relationship was with a guy who was physically, verbally and mentally abusive.
- She met "the love of her life," but it just didn't seem right, so she didn't stay with him.
- Her next partner was insecure and controlling, and took no interest in their baby.
- She reconnected with "the love of her life," who be-

trayed her over and over for the next seven years.

Can you imagine the breadth and depth of Sam's emotional wounds? These wounds are the reason why Sam keeps running into sociopaths.

Human energy fields

What exactly is an emotional wound? It is a disturbance in our own personal energy field. These disturbances affect our health and our lives until they are healed.

I'm going to briefly explain how it works. I'm not an expert in this. But I can say that if I didn't have my energy healer, it would have been much more difficult for me to recover from the experience of being betrayed by my sociopathic ex-husband. (If you'd like to know more about my experience, I explain it in detail in my first book, *Love Fraud*.)

Much of today's understanding of energy medicine is based on ancient Indian and Chinese concepts. The foundation is the idea that a life force, or energy, permeates the entire universe and everything in it, including us. This energy is called "prana" in Sanskrit and "chi" or "qi" by the Chinese. (Many other cultures also recognize this energy.)

Our personal energy fields include several distinct structures. The most well-known are the meridians used in acupuncture and acupressure, the seven chakras and the aura, which itself has seven distinct layers.

Some well-known healers, such as Donna Eden and Barbara Brennan, can perceive these energy fields. My energy healer could also see my chakras and aura. Barbara Brennan (who earned degrees in physics and atmospheric physics and worked for NASA) believes anyone can learn to perceive them.

Energy disturbances

An interview with Barbara Brennan, *Exploring the Human Energy System* on Healthy.net, explains how our human energy fields work.

On page 2 of the story, about halfway down, the interviewer,

Russel E. DiCarlo, asks Brennan:

> You have said that the major cause of illness stems from how we habitually imbalance our fields, thereby making it weak and ourselves susceptible to physical illness. Why do we do this?

Brennan explains that when we experience childhood traumas, disturbances are created in our energy fields. I would add that these energetic disturbances are created any time during our lives when we experience trauma, disappointment or betrayal.

We don't want to feel the pain of our experiences, Brennan explains. "So we create a way to hold these 'blobs,' shall we say, of consciousness and energy so that we might never have to experience them." Consequently, the disturbances get stuck in our energy fields.

These stuck disturbances have two effects:

- They create blockages that prevent our life energies from flowing properly.
- They draw more experiences to our lives that match the energy of the disturbance.

This is exactly what is happening to Sam. She had one abusive experience after another in her life. With this parade of sociopaths, the energy disturbances they caused are likely still stuck in her energy field.

Energy attracts energy that is like itself. So because of the energy disturbances caused by sociopaths, more sociopaths keep showing up.

This, of course, is painful. But in the next question of the interview, Brennan explains that pain motivates us to change.

Healing the disturbances

So how do we get the disturbances out of our energy fields? One way is to allow ourselves to actually feel the pain and trauma of the experiences.

Often we're afraid of the pain. We feel that if we ever allow ourselves to start crying about what happened to us, or if we pull the lid off of our anger, the emotions will overwhelm us.

But keeping the pain bottled up becomes toxic. It prevents us from enjoying life as we should. It also turns into disease, such as cancer.

I believe we should allow ourselves to cry. We should express our anger, although not necessarily to the person who betrayed us. That's useless with a sociopath. It's much better to take out your anger on a punching bag.

Another way to dissolve the negative energy is through EFT tapping. I recently wrote about this in, *True recovery from the sociopath through tapping and energy psychology.*

Sam, I recommend that you work on your personal healing. By siphoning off the negative energy and replacing it with positive energy, you'll change your life.

More information

Some people believe these ideas are New Age hocus pocus. But scientists have recently been able to measure and document the effects of universal energy and the human energy field. Here are some books that I've found helpful in explaining these concepts. They're all available on Amazon.com.

Hands of Light — A guide to healing through the human energy field, by Barbara Ann Brennan, Ph.D.

Energy Medicine and Energy Medicine for Women, by Donna Eden and David Feinstein.

The Genie in Your Genes — epigenetic medicine and the new biology of intention, by Dawson Church, Ph.D.

The Promise of Energy Psychology — Revolutionary tools for dramatic personal change, by David Feinstein, Donna Eden and Gary Craig.

Breaking the compulsion to fix and help

Lovefraud received the following letter from a reader whom we'll call "Emilie."

I won't go into the long, boring details of my 7+ year relationship with the sociopath that invaded my life. It's the same basic story as always and plus, I think there's some kind of email size limit. :)

Ever since I ended the engagement over 3 years ago, and finally terminated the relationship itself another year after, I've made comments (in a lighthearted, self deprecating fashion) that, "If you're going to treat me like crap, then I'm the girl for you!" Yes, it gets chuckles from the people I'm around, but sadly it's true.

I was watching a movie last night and was judging the characters on their level of attractiveness, which was directly proportional to their level of emotional damage. It started off as a fun little game — and then it hit me. It's really not a game. It really isn't a flippant remark. I seriously cannot be attracted to someone unless they're damaged! What. The. Hell!

It occurred to me while I was drifting off to sleep (what I call the "brain cleaning" portion of the verge of deep sleep), that even in my mid-twenties (am creeping up on my mid-forties now), my stepmother made the comment to me that I do that. Even then, I went for the boys that needed to be fixed or helped. It's no wonder that I was such a perfect target for the two sociopaths that jacked up my life. Actually I'm kind of surprised it hasn't been more!

Okay — back to my point. After so long of being alone, about a year ago I tried to be in a relationship. It did not work out well. He was a nice enough guy, but GOD was he clingy and needy! Holy crap! He was nice to play with for a couple of weeks, but I soon perceived he was trying to control me. I say perceived. In all fairness, he might not have been trying to control me, but it felt that way (constricting), so I got the hell out of Dodge!

So here I am. Alone. And basically okay with that. It's much less risky to be alone, and to be honest, the very thought of entering into a relationship of the romantic persuasion scares the holy bejesus out of me. Like, it gives me real anxiety. But, damn — sometimes it'd be nice — PLUS the fact that, okay, so, you can't help who you're attracted to, right? I mean, isn't that just biology or physiology or something?

Since I have this predilection to be attracted to the damaged, how can I break out of this? I can't trust myself at all. At this point, I can only assume that if I am attracted to someone, there is something fundamentally wrong with him. I'm no expert, but that's pretty morbid.

Is there a way to change this, or is this something I'm just going to have to live with being aware of?

Donna Andersen responds

Dear Emilie,

You should congratulate yourself. You have just taken the first step toward understanding why the sociopaths, and other partners who treated you badly, have shown up in your life.

Usually there is a purpose for our nasty encounters with sociopaths. We hate to admit it. We don't want to give these exploiters, these predators, credit for anything worthwhile. But generally the object of the exercise, the reason we're involved with them, is to draw our attention to something within us that needs to be healed.

Sociopaths hook us by targeting our vulnerabilities. By identifying how they snagged us, we identify those vulnerabilities. And once we know what they are, we can work towards healing them.

So now you know. You have a "predilection to be attracted to the damaged." The question is, why? Why do you feel compelled to rescue people? Why do you expect to give, while your partners take?

Looking for reasons

Sometimes the answer is in our family of origin. If you grew up with disordered parents, for example, you may have learned that your survival depended on taking care of them or keeping them happy.

Sometimes our upbringing and early life were fairly normal, but we still managed to absorb unhealthy beliefs. Maybe you have a deep, hidden belief that you must take care of other people, but you can't expect other people to take care of you.

There is a vulnerability, a lack, a wound, within you, which the sociopath and other exploiters sensed. Now you have to figure out what it is.

Answers are within

How do you do that? You ask yourself. Your inner self, or higher self, knows the answer. You just need to ask, and listen.

You can do this as an exercise. Sit quietly with a pad of paper and a pen. Then ask yourself, "Why am I attracted to damaged men?" A response will pop into your head. Write it down. Ask yourself the question again, and another response will pop into your head. Write it down. Keep doing this, and you'll get a whole list of reasons. Some may not be useful. But one or two of them will reveal your core unhealthy beliefs.

You can then explore those unhealthy beliefs further. Suppose one of your answers was, "I don't deserve a healthy partner." Ask yourself, "Why don't I deserve a healthy partner?" Again, write down the response.

After a while, you may discover a whole list of beliefs that you didn't know you had.

Releasing the beliefs

Now what? What do you do with all the beliefs? You release them.

Here's a way to do it. State your negative belief as a positive belief. For example, say to yourself, "Of course I deserve a healthy partner." As you do this, notice how you feel.

You may feel fear. Or disappointment. Or pain. If something inside you resists your positive belief, you know you've hit pay dirt.

Allow yourself to feel the resistance. Bring it to your awareness. Your objective is to feel the emotion that underlies your beliefs, and let it go. The emotion is the energetic charge that keeps the unhealthy beliefs alive. When you release the emotion, you can change your beliefs as well.

I've written on many occasions about making the decision to recover from your experience with the sociopath. This is what I mean. Actively go looking for those beliefs and decisions within you that have made you vulnerable. Once you find and release them, you'll be on your way to recovery.

At some point, a healthy individual will be standing in front of you, and you'll be ready.

How to dump a sociopath

Suppose you realize that you're in an unhealthy romantic relationship. Or, your instincts are telling you that the person in hot pursuit of you is bad news. How do you end the involvement?

When you're romantically involved with reasonably normal individuals, you usually try to spare their feelings. You don't come out and say that they're boring, or needy, or oafish, even if that's what you feel. You make up excuses. You tell them that you're getting back with an old boyfriend or girlfriend, even if that's a lie. You say you're just not ready for a relationship right now, even if that's also a lie.

In essence, when breaking up with an okay person who just isn't your type, you try to let them down easy.

This is precisely the wrong approach when breaking up with a sociopath.

Red Flags of Lovefraud

Perhaps this hot new lover has swept into your life, showered you with attention and affection, and is promising a wonderful future. Initially, you are swept off your feet, head-over-heels excited.

But, because you're a Lovefraud reader, you eventually recognize this person's inordinate attention as love bombing. You look for the other Red Flags of Love Fraud, and you see them.

In the meantime, your instincts have been trying to get your attention. You've been ignoring them, but you no longer can. You've seen the mask slip. There was a flicker of rage, or manipulation, or cold indifference. And this person is slowly trying to control you, under the guise of concern for your welfare, or wanting to be with you every moment of every day.

You finally admit to yourself that this is a bad situation, and you need to end it.

What do you do?

Rejection statement

The following advice applies if you're in a relationship that does not include complications such as kids, property or massive amounts of money.

Tell the person ONE TIME that you do not want any involvement with him or her. Make your decision very clear.

In my *Love Fraud and How to Avoid It* presentation, I teach students the following rejection statement. It's based on the recommended statement in *The Gift of Fear,* by Gavin DeBecker.

> I have no romantic interest in you whatsoever.
> I am certain I never will.
> Do not contact me ever again.

Yes, it's brutal. Don't worry about hurting their feelings. Remember, if you're dealing with a sociopath, he or she doesn't really have any. You want to make it very clear that you want nothing to do with this person.

By the way, yes, you can send the rejection statement via text or email. It's safer for you, because if you're not physically there, the person does not have the opportunity to manipulate you.

No Contact

After you tell the person ONE TIME that you do not want an involvement, you have no further contact with this individual.

You do not talk on the phone.

You do not send texts or emails.

You certainly do not see the individual in person.

You do not visit their Facebook page.

Some sociopaths will immediately start a campaign to win you back. They'll call, text and email incessantly. DO NOT RESPOND.

If the person sends you 50 text messages, and after the 51st text message, you reply saying, "Leave me alone," you have taught the person that it takes 50 text messages to get a response from you. So they start sending messages again.

There are several approaches to avoiding messages from the sociopath. You can block calls and text messages on your phone, or change your phone number. You can block emails or change your email address. The downside of these approaches is that the sociopath knows he or she is being blocked, and will try to circumvent your efforts.

Gavin DeBecker suggests another approach. He advises you to keep the phone number that the sociopath knows, but get another line. Give the new number to the people who you want to have it. The sociopath keeps calling, but the calls go to voice mail, which you never check. The benefit of this approach is that the sociopath believes the calls are going through, and you are ignoring them.

Physical danger

If the sociopath has been violent towards you, you need to be extra cautious. The most dangerous time for anyone in a violent relationship if right when you leave. The abuser will be angry about losing control over you and may strike out.

If the sociopath has not been violent towards you, but you know he or she has been violent towards other people, animals or property, you should still be cautious. Any history of violence is an indication that the violence could be turned towards you.

Therefore, use extra caution when ending the involvement with someone who is violent. If you are living together, leave when the person is not home. Ask your family and friends for support. You may need to contact the police.

The return

When you tell them that the involvement is over, some sociopaths will leave you alone for awhile. Then, after weeks, months or even years, they return.

They admit that they were wrong in the relationship. They tell you that they've been to therapy, or to church. They say you were the best thing that ever happened to them, and they want to try again.

Do not fall for it. Sooner or later, you'll see the same controlling or abusive behavior as before — except it will be worse. And you, having taken them back, will have less emotional strength to throw them out again.

Dumping the sociopath

This is the basic outline for dumping the sociopath. It may need to be modified based on your situation — it's more difficult, for example, if you and your ex-partner work together. (In that case, you may need to look for a new job.)

Here are the key points:

- Tell the person ONE TIME that you want no involvement.
- Then, have NO CONTACT with the person.

Remember, No Contact is vital. It ends your involvement, and enables you to recover.

10 lessons from the mistakes we made with sociopaths

Many years ago, I attended a workshop presented by Patricia Sun, a pioneer of the self-awareness movement. One of the things she talked about was shifting our views about making mistakes.

We tend to fear making mistakes, and when we do make mistakes, we berate ourselves. But in reality, mistakes are a part of life. There are no instruction manuals for most of the choices we make. Life, therefore, is a series of decisions made mostly by trial and error. We never progress in a straight line towards out goals. We have false starts and detours, but with time and persistence, we get to where we want to go.

Patricia Sun talked about viewing mistakes as opportunities to make course corrections. The energy associated with making a mistake, she says, should be that of a learning opportunity, an indication that a change is required to achieve our goals.

Mistakes with sociopaths

What would happen if this were how we viewed the mistakes we made with sociopaths? Instead of feeling like a chump, like the biggest idiot on the planet, what if we looked at our encounters as identifying needed course corrections?

Here are 10 of the lessons we've learned. Can you add any to the list?

1. Wow — I sure don't want that kind of a partner.

2. I had no idea people like this existed.
3. Yes — some people can look me right in the eye and lie.
4. I knew something was off — I have to listen to myself.
5. Some people are not capable of being a loving parent.
6. I deserve better than this.
7. When I see this type of behavior, I have to run, and run fast.
8. Certain people cannot be trusted and will not change.
9. When I'm vulnerable, I need to protect myself.
10. When some people say, "I love you," they mean, "I want to use you."

Best decisions at the time

None of us intentionally signs up to be exploited by a sociopath. What happened was that we didn't know what sociopaths looked like, and we met someone who deceived us.

If the sociopath was a romantic partner, at first, he or she seemed like the person we'd been waiting for all our lives. It was only later, once we were hooked into a relationship, that the person's true character was revealed.

The involvement was a mistake. But mistakes are apparent only in hindsight.

So I think we should cut ourselves some slack. Then we should look at the experience, figure out what we learned, and apply the lessons to the rest of our lives.

Pain as motivation for
freeing yourself from sociopaths

An article on Lovefraud is entitled, *Healing your addiction to sociopaths.* In it, I offer three steps for changing a pattern of falling in love with sociopaths. The steps are:

- No Contact with the current sociopath
- Do not date anyone for the time being
- Heal the vulnerabilities

The real work is in the third step — healing your vulnerabilities. What I suggest sounds somewhat like the good advice that we get on many topics, like:

- Eat your vegetables
- Make time for regular exercise
- Cut down on sugar, carbs and alcohol
- Get enough sleep

We all know we should do all these things, but do we do them? How often do we skip going to the gym, or pour ourselves another glass of wine?

So why should "healing our vulnerabilities" be any different? What would make us put time and energy into this "good for you" program, when we slide on so many others?

The answer is the emotional pain we feel due to the sociopath.

Motivation to recover

Just as physical pain is a symptom that something is wrong with our body, emotional pain is a symptom that something is wrong with our internal self. The pain can be so searing, and so devastating, that how we respond to it affects our very survival. Either we find a way to alleviate the pain, or we die if not a literal death, then the death of our spirit.

If you are feeling the pain of sociopathic betrayal, channel that pain into motivation. Use the pain as motivation to recover from not only the most recent experience, but to seek out and cure the internal vulnerabilities that made you fall for the sociopath in the first place.

Mistaken beliefs

Usually these vulnerabilities are mistaken beliefs about our own worthiness, lovability and place in the world. We may have absorbed these beliefs from the sociopaths, from our parents and family of origin, or from society in general. Recognizing and releasing false, harmful beliefs enables us to change our lives.

I recognize that this is not easy and it takes time. But once you get to the other side of the process, you'll find the peace, stability, and perhaps even the relationship, you always wanted. I know I did.

We are all worthy. We all deserve love, starting with self-love. There can be a benefit to the sociopathic pain — an opportunity to make these truths part of our being.

Recovery: parallel courses for moving forward

What sociopaths do to us is unfair, coercive, exploitative and evil. In a just world, they would be held accountable. They would be forced to return what they took from us, and compensate us for the pain and suffering they have caused. They might even be prosecuted and imprisoned.

But we do not live in a just world. We live in a world that is oblivious to the human predators among us. We live in a world where clueless people believe a convincing liar; the best performer wins and courts have neither the time nor the inclination to sort out the truth from the lies.

For all of us who have been targeted, this adds insult to injury. We've been abused and exploited. We are damaged. Then because we are damaged, we are at a disadvantage when we seek redress —and this just adds to the damage.

Even when we do prevail, it can be a hollow victory. When I divorced my ex-husband, James Montgomery, I won in court. The judge found that my ex committed fraud. I was awarded everything that was taken from me — $227,000 — plus $1 million in punitive damages.

I then spent thousands of dollars hiring a private investigator and lawyers to track down my ex, because I was sure he had money — money that was rightfully mine. I failed, and in the end I had to declare bankruptcy.

Parallel courses

Here's where many of us make a big mistake: We believe that the successful resolution of the crisis caused by the sociopath will lead to our healing.

In reality, solving the problems caused by the sociopath and working towards personal recovery are two separate pursuits. To reclaim our life, we need to move forward along two parallel courses:

- Dealing with the real-world situation that we face
- Pursuing physical, psychological and emotional healing

The good news with this realization is that we don't have to wait until the situation with the sociopath is resolved in order to begin our personal recovery. We can start taking care our health. We can overcome our addiction to the relationship and begin deeper healing.

Think of the implications of this understanding. We no longer have to put our life and recovery on hold, waiting for the sociopath to face justice — justice that may never come. Dealing with the sociopath becomes a project in our lives, like cleaning out the garage. It's something we do. It is not who we are.

Our true, important effort is our personal recovery and growth — and we can work on this regardless of what happens to the sociopath.

Decisions about fixing the situation

To decide what actions to take or how to respond to the sociopath, we have to evaluate both parallel courses for moving forward, and the interplay between them.

To deal with the situation, we need a very clear understanding of the personality disorder — Lovefraud has plenty of information on that. With this understanding, and our knowledge of the individual, we can probably begin to anticipate what the sociopath will do. In deciding how to proceed, we also need to evaluate our resources and possible outcomes of different courses of actions.

At the same time, we need to consider our personal recovery. Where are we emotionally and psychologically? How much can we tolerate? What actions — or lack of actions — would be most beneficial to our own recovery?

I don't advocate that everyone simply cut their losses and run. Sometimes the more you give in to the sociopath, the more he or she demands, so it may be critical to fight. Or, what we really need for our personal recovery is to take a stand for ourselves, not allowing ourselves to be trampled again. I, personally, am very glad that I pursued my ex in court. Even though I never got any money, the court's finding of fraud is what enabled me to launch Lovefraud. I had proof that he was a con artist.

In deciding how to best move forward, all of us targeted by sociopaths should balance the two parallel courses for moving forward: The reality of our situation and our own personal recovery.

Relationships after the sociopath

I received the following email from the Lovefraud reader who posts as "Zimzoomit:"

> I saw the Lifetime Network show about you and love-fraud.com. What I would like to know is how the man who came next (your true lover, after the fraud) helped you to overcome the emotional havoc your ex who frauded you caused? Is there a specific blog or link on lovefraud.com to tell us how he helped you?
>
> Were you able to talk about things that bothered you about your ex, even ever so occasionally, when/if the haunted thoughts encroached on you — even if only occasionally but for years after the fact, and if so, what things did your new love say, to help you overcome those thoughts? Was he willing to listen, or did he occasionally treat you like a "broken record"?

Yes, after the sociopath, I now have a wonderful husband, Terry Kelly. We truly love each other, care about each other, and want each other to be happy. I should point out, however, that Terry wasn't my first relationship after the con artist.

First post-sociopath relationship

Seven months after I left my sociopathic husband, James Montgomery, I started dating a man named John. John was younger than me, fun and entertaining. We actually met online and corresponded for more than two months before meeting in person.

At the time, I was in the midst of finding out what my ex was really all about, communicating with some of his other victims, and filing for divorce. I described some of what was going on in my emails. The story, of course, was outrageous, and I guess that John was actually intrigued.

John lived an hour and 45 minutes away from me, so we saw each other only on weekends. We did normal dating things — going out to dinner, to concerts, to parties with his friends or my friends. That's one of the biggest things John offered me — a sense of normalcy, like a safe harbor amid the insanity of my divorce. He also paid for all our entertainment, which I appreciated, because I was broke.

I did talk to him about my outrage at my ex and my frustration with the legal case. John stayed with me until the divorce was finalized, and for a few months after that. Eventually, however, the relationship ended, and he did make a comment to the effect of, "all you talk about is James." He may have also begun to feel that my problems were just too big, and he couldn't solve them.

Still, we had loved each other, and because I loved him, the end of the relationship was emotionally more painful than the end of my marriage. In retrospect, however, John and I were really quite different, not an ideal match. I believe that John was in my life to support me at a very difficult time — and that was it. I have fond memories of him, but our relationship was not meant to be forever.

Second post-sociopath relationship

Ten months after I broke up with John, I met Terry at a nightclub. A week or so later he took me out to dinner, and we talked about our circumstances. He had been in a long-term marriage, and his wife had just asked for a divorce. I figured I might as well be honest, and told him that I was married to a con man who took a quarter million dollars from me, cheated with multiple women, etc., etc.

I didn't know how Terry was going to react. In fact, a month passed before he called for another date — I thought I had scared him away. But when he arrived for our second date, he brought his most recent tax return to show me. He thought what I had been through was terrible, and wanted to show me that he did make his own money.

Terry and I dated for four years before we married. With him, I truly learned to give and receive love, and live in partnership. We care about and support each other. He's my biggest cheerleader with Lovefraud. In fact, I couldn't have created it without his support.

If you'd like to read more about how these men helped me, it's all in the printed edition of my first book, *Love Fraud — how marriage to a sociopath fulfilled my spiritual plan.* (The e-book has been abridged, and does not contain the description of my relationship with John.) The story really is romantic.

Primer for post-sociopath relationships

Here are what I think are the take-home lessons:

1. In order to have a happy, loving relationship with someone else, we must first heal ourselves.

No one can overcome the emotional havoc for us — we must do it ourselves. While I was dating both John and Terry, I was also working with my energy counselor to release all of the pain of the betrayal by my sociopathic ex. Then, I had to work with her to release the emotional pain of losing the relationship with John. By the time I met Terry, I had made a lot of progress, so I was in a much better place to build a solid relationship.

2. Sometimes we find interim relationships before we find true love.

Not every relationship is meant to be permanent. Sometimes we just travel life's journey together for awhile, supporting each other in some way, then our journeys diverge. This was my experience with John. Although I was sad when the relationship ended, I eventually realized that it had been exactly what I needed at the time. It was perfect.

3. Real love is easy.

In a true loving relationship, there are no games, no power plays, and no exploitation. There is an honest give and take. The two people in the relationship truly care about the each other's welfare, happiness and success. Real love is peaceful and easy.

Terry and I have been together for years, and I'm still excited to see him. We still make each other laugh; we still want to snuggle. But if I hadn't done all the internal work that I did, I'm not sure if I would have been able to experience such a wonderful love.

The relationship we experience always depends on what is going on inside of us. That's why it's so important to make a decision to heal, and then do what it takes to rebuild ourselves.

Sociopaths leave us totally disoriented — here's why

Most of us grow up believing that all people are created equal, that human beings are basically good, and everybody wants to be loved. These are the messages we learn in school, in church, and in the age of political correctness, from the media.

These beliefs are the lenses through which we view the world and the people in it. Our beliefs influence how we perceive and understand the behavior of those we meet. And, for 88 percent of the population, the beliefs work just fine.

Bad treatment

Then we realize that someone in our life isn't treating us well. We may think this person is reacting to our behavior, that we're doing something to provoke anger or elicit criticism — after all, that's what we're told.

We know we're not actually doing what we're accused of doing, so we try to figure out where the outbursts and hostility are coming from — did he or she have a difficult childhood? Is he or she still suffering from the pain of a former relationship?

We try to understand and accept. We stop asking questions; we stop doing things that "push buttons." But nothing changes. In fact, we're treated worse than ever.

So we take to the Internet to find out the reason for the behavior. We Google "pathological lying" or "domestic abuse" or "cheating." Or, we describe our experiences to a friend, and our friend says, "It sounds like a sociopath."

We find a checklist of sociopathic behavior, and, to our shock and dismay, it exactly describes the person who is causing us so much pain.

Why do they do it?

I can't tell you how many times Lovefraud readers have told me stories that follow this basic outline. When I talk to people on the phone, the question I hear most often is, "Why do they do that?"

- Why do they lie, even when they'd be better off telling the truth?
- Why do they blame me for everything?
- Why won't they let me go, when they're already seeing someone else?
- Why are they telling everyone that I'm mentally unbalanced?
- Why do they want to ruin me?

The answer to these questions is: They act this way because they're sociopaths, and that's what sociopaths do.

Shattering beliefs

Learning that sociopaths exist is like an earthquake, a tsunami, for our belief system.

Our ideas that that all people are created equal, that human beings are basically good, and that everybody wants to be loved are not totally correct. Yes, these ideas apply to most people in the human race — but not everyone. A certain percentage of the people who live among us are fundamentally different, rotten to the core, and unable to love.

This is why experiences with sociopaths are so disorienting. Not only have we suffered physical, financial, emotional or psychological abuse, but we are also forced to accept that our entire understanding of life and other people is flawed.

This is why we feel like the rug has been pulled out from under us. This is why we feel like we cannot trust ourselves. Realizing that social predators live among us causes our worldview to collapse.

What we have learned, through painful experience, is that there are exceptions to what we previously believed. We now know that there are people who look just like us and act just like us — at least when we first meet them. But their objective is not to live alongside us; instead, they want to exploit us.

We now know that sociopaths exist. With this information we can modify our worldview, realizing that we must carefully evaluate every person that we let into our lives.

What we should do when sociopaths experience no consequences

Lovefraud recently received the following email from a reader who posts as "Salvation2012."

Thank you for helping me decide when I needed to cut my losses during my divorce. I did cut my "losses," yet the total I received tallied up to a number similar, just not in all cash. Because I settled in his eyes, he told everyone I was just proving how I was the guilty one and didn't want to risk being exposed. To the end he will deny permanently injuring me and bleeding me of money, and cheating on me (which I only later found out about the extent).

My recent concern is watching him seemingly have no consequences. I'm not a vengeful person, so this is a distressing area for me, but I just thought karma or something would move in. How was he convicted of a crime, and given no contact and stay away orders from civil and criminal courts, and still have his job, and still be with the woman he was with (apparently for the last 7 years. We were together since January 2007, so their relationship lasted the entirety of our time together), and his friends are happy for him.

Maybe I'm staunch in my morals, but if I had a friend who was found guilty and the judge took away his first time offenders rights because 1) the severity of the injuries and 2) it was only the first caught act of violence, I would not support that person anymore. I would say that person dug themselves a big hole and it's theirs to climb out of or stay in.

I am finding peace in my new location, yet struggle with reality checking and normal people actually being normal and trusting that. He seems to be just fine and has announced to all the love of his life, and he is finally happy happy happy, and has been with her since last May, which was while we were still married, and is the incorrect start date — as her husband contacted me and has been following them for 7 years of his marriage (they are now going through a divorce).

It's not a jealousy, but an envy of how he is so unaffected by what he did to me, even with law and court representatives telling him to his face what they saw in him. I don't want to have to figure him out anymore as it prevents me from fully moving forward. So how do I turn off the switch when the spath is moving on easily and I am still finding my ground?

Salvation2012 brings up two issues here that seem to be intertwined, but they really aren't. The issues are what happens to the sociopath, and what happens to us.

The sociopath

Chances are very good that sooner or later, karma will move in on the sociopath. At some point sociopaths usually screw up. They go too far over the line, anger the wrong person, get sloppy, run out of people to exploit, or suffer medical consequences after years of unhealthy living.

But this is not going to happen on our timetable. In fact, we may never even hear of the sociopath's unseemly collapse.

In the meantime, sociopaths seem to be getting away with everything. And yes, they are unaffected. But think about why they are unaffected: They are hollow, empty shells of human beings. They have no heart and no conscience. This is what enables them to shred us and move on without a second thought.

I'd rather keep my heart and conscience and suffer the pain

than live their eternally barren existence.

So what do we do? We let them go. We let go of our experience with them. Our goal should be to get to the point where they simply don't matter. They are non-entities.

Our own path of healing

Letting go of the sociopath is actually one of the best things we can do for ourselves. When we stop worrying, or even wondering, about consequences for the sociopath, we can focus our energy on our own healing.

Salvation2012 asked, "How do I turn off the switch?"

The first step is to viscerally accept what happened to us. Usually the switch that connects us to the sociopath is jammed on because we're still beating ourselves up for falling for the lies, or wishing that what happened in our life did not happen.

We don't condone the actions of the sociopath. We don't like what happened, either. But we do have to get to the point where we can say, "It happened, and there's nothing I can do about that now, except move forward."

Then we take steps to process the pain. We look for our vulnerabilities and address them, so that we never fall for a sociopath again. And as we go along, we make sure to be good to ourselves.

Yes, we were hurt, but that's because we have a heart and a conscience — both of which we want to cherish.

5 steps to get the sociopath out of your head

Ionce heard from a woman whom we'll call "Rochelle." When Rochelle was in her 50s, through a high school reunion, she reconnected with the first boy she ever loved. Rochelle had a crush on him when she was 14. They dated for almost five years, although he always seemed to have an eye out for other girls. When they broke up, Rochelle was heartbroken, but she moved on, married, divorced, and life was reasonably good — until that first love came back into her life.

He poured on the charm, and Rochelle felt like finally, after more than 30 years, she had her chance to be with the guy she always wanted. Rochelle left everything to move out of state with him. They eventually married.

Well, he lied, fabricated, manipulated, accused, took her money, ruined her credit, filed for divorce behind her back, and left her with nothing. It was the type of behavior we all know so well — sociopathic behavior.

Rochelle realizes that the guy is disordered; she was exploited; he never loved her. Still, she wants him. Yet she also realizes that she's in love with a person who does not exist.

She asks, "When does it get to the point where he stops taking up space in my brain?"

Scope of the question

The first thing to understand is the scope of this question. "Getting the sociopath out of my head" is the ultimate goal of everyone who has been betrayed by one of these predators. Once you've achieved it, you've achieved full recovery.

So cut yourself some slack. This individual probably crashed through your life like a battering ram. Your emotions, finances, home, health and/or psyche may all be in splinters. This is going to take time to repair. If anyone says to you, "Just get over it," this person has no idea what you're experiencing.

1. Understand what happened

You were probably blindsided by this experience, so in order to move forward, you need to understand what happened. We have lots of material here on Lovefraud to help you. Many people have told me that my two books, *Love Fraud* and *Red Flags of Love Fraud*, were especially helpful.

Here are some key concepts:

- **Sociopaths exist.** They are social predators and they live their lives by exploiting people. They do not feel remorse for their actions, and they will never change.
- **The sociopath never loved you.** You were targeted because you had something he or she wanted. It could have been money, sex, a place to live, business connections or cover for his or her secret life. Or, the sociopath messed with you simply for the fun of it.
- **There is nothing you could have done to make the sociopath treat you any better.** The involvement was always about exploitation. You were probably targeted because you were good, caring, giving, responsible, and in some way, vulnerable.
- **The blame for what happened rests squarely with the sociopath.** This person lied to you, manipulated you and betrayed you. You were guilty only of being human.

2. Acceptance

Recovering from sociopaths is a process. The key to the process is accepting what happened. This does not mean that you excuse what happened, or that you try to forgive and forget. But you must believe that yes, he or she did it, and yes, the sociopath knew what he or she was doing.

You can't make time go backwards. You can't take back the things you said or did that enabled the sociopath to become part of your life.

Once you come to terms with the fact that yes, it did happen, you begin the healing process.

3. Addictive relationship

In the case I described at the beginning of the article, Rochelle said that she still wanted the sociopath. This is not quite accurate. The truth is that she was addicted to him.

Relationships with sociopaths are highly addictive. They actually cause chemical and structural changes in the brain, similar to what substance addictions do. Therefore, you need to treat leaving the sociopath like kicking an addiction.

The way to do this is to have no further contact with this individual—no phone calls, no email, no text messages. Certainly do not meet the person. Don't even go to the individual's Facebook page.

If you must have contact with the individual for some reason — like you have a child together — do your best to implement Emotional No Contact. That means you remain absolutely neutral in any interaction. Sociopath love to get emotional reactions from their targets, and will do whatever they can to engage you. Do not take the bait.

Staying away from the sociopath can be really difficult. But the longer you stay away, the stronger you'll become. If you give in and have contact, you'll have to start all over again.

4. Processing the pain

This was not a normal relationship, and it's not a normal break-up. Even if you weren't physically or sexually assaulted, you suffered massive emotional and psychic injuries. You have losses that need to be grieved, including your loss of trust.

I believe that you must allow yourself to feel the pain of the experience, although you may not be able to do this right away. In the beginning you may just be numb. This a protective measure taken by your psyche, because the injury is just so massive.

Eventually, you need to let yourself feel it. You cannot bottle the pain up within you. It will either poison your life, or it will make you ill. You must get the pain out of your system.

Cry your eyes out. Stomp you feet in anger. Take up boxing and hit a punching bag. It's scary at first to face your own anger, embarrassment, rage, humiliation — whatever the sociopath caused. But allow yourself to feel the emotions, honor them, and then let them go.

5. Let joy into your life

Draining the negative emotions will leave an energetic void within you. How do you fill the empty space? You allow joy into your life.

Any kind of joy will do: Enjoying a sunny day, letting your pets comfort you, having coffee with a friend, letting a waitress be nice to you. Soak up any joy and pleasantness that you encounter.

As you drain the negative emotions, and replace them with instances of joy, you'll slowly change your perspective. Gradually, you'll find that the sociopath is no longer renting space in your head. And that's what you want to achieve.

What feels like pain is really progress

Lovefraud recently received the following letter from a reader whom we'll call "Cassandra." My reply follows the letter.

I don't even know where to begin but I'll try and make it short. Won't be sweet though.

I am a long time advocate of Lovefraud. I was a victim of a psychopath over 7 years ago. I was with him for 5 years, we had a house together, dogs, like a married couple. Finally a girl confronted me and told me he was living a double life, as well as having sex with both men and women. And I was not shocked. Just angry at myself for not facing the truth for so long. I ended the relationship. He tried to get me back. I got a restraining order. To this day he still tries to email and call me every few months. I've accepted that I will have to deal with that for the rest of my life.

Fast forward to now. It has been 3 years since I have even considered dating, or even touching a man. I am a brilliant career woman. I am successful, make decent money — and live totally alone. I am scared of men, afraid to date, but am getting tired of not having any male companionship. So, for the first time in 3 years since I was with the psychopath, I went out on a date. First time.

It was an incredible date. Gorgeous guy, even though he looked like a computer nerd. Glasses, Jewish, intellectual, shy, artistic and unfortunately the kind of man I crave. Incredible connection, incredible sex, and I was the one in fact telling him that we needed to take this slower. Except he knew exactly what to do. Constant texts, wanting to see me immediately the next day, insisting that he wanted a relationship with me and then changing his tune an hour later saying he wasn't sure, etc.

At first, I was disgusted and knew I didn't need any of this crap. I called him on the bluff and told him let's just back off. 24 hours later, I was the one wondering what he was doing and where he was. He would say "I'm going to see you this afternoon," and then he wouldn't show. I would get a text at 10 pm saying his brother was in the hospital and perhaps I am available "tomorrow?" I would fret and stress, wondering if my own paranoia was keeping me from trusting this individual, and that this certainly couldn't happen to me two times in a row that I would date a psychopath. So I gave him the benefit of the doubt and said sure. The next day he did not show. He texted again saying something came up but he'd love to see me that night. With false hope, I agreed but didn't bet on it.

That night, I was more anxious and worried than ever before. I sat there on my couch, the house all cleaned, the fire going, a perfect romantic atmosphere. I sat there, and 9 pm came and went. I called and texted "Are you on your way?" No response. At 10 pm I turned off the music, the lights, and found myself just staring at the fireplace. I was in what I call a shock of realization.

I turned off the lights, went to bed, lay there until 2 am. At some point I just broke and cried.

Donna, I wasn't even looking for this. I was not even looking for someone to suddenly "love" me. I just wanted to meet someone who would appreciate who I was on the inside, without being impressed by my career. I just wanted a night — just one night — of being with a man and having good conversation, good talk, and affection. And that one person that I reached out to after years and years of not dating due to being with a psychopath turned out to be another one.

I woke up this morning with my eyes hurting from crying and just drained, as if I have been up for weeks without any sleep. I got up, did coffee, lay on the couch and suddenly broke down and sobbed again. And I can't help but sob to myself, even though I know I shouldn't, that "I'm so stupid." I am so stupid. I am so stupid. I absolutely hate myself right now, and I hate that I am talented. I hate that I am successful. I hate that I am pretty. I hate that I am a target. I hate that I can't relate to anyone with the lonely road I take with work. I hate that I am not understood. And most especially, I hate that a psychopath got me the minute I snuck out of my hole after three years.

Now I'm back in the hole. Feeling stupid. Feeling more alone than before. And more hopeless than before. And that I gave all my built up talent and energy to a stranger that got drunk off it, and is doing god knows what with it right now to someone else.

I hope to get over this again as well, but I can't stop crying and I can't stop staring at the floor and just whispering, I'm so stupid.

Am I destined to be alone? Working career woman, never being appreciated for who she is on the inside and only being admired on the outside? That means nothing to me. And the minute that I show my true self, it's a psychopath that eats it up. Why am I here on this planet if this is always going to be the case?

Donna Andersen responds

Dear Cassandra,

I am so very sorry that, on the very first time you looked for companionship again, you ran into another psychopath. It is so painful. I know exactly how you feel, because I've been there, or at least someplace similar. It really hurts.

You demand of yourself, the universe or whatever higher power you believe in, "Why me? What did I do wrong? Why did this happen again? How long will this go on? Haven't I paid enough? Am I destined to remain alone and unloved for the rest of my life? Why can't I catch a break? When will it be over?

I'd like to offer a different perspective of your most recent experience: I think you're making progress.

Here is what has happened: You were ready to take the next step in your healing. And that step was to access, and excavate, the residual pain still buried within you from your first psychopathic ex. Or, perhaps there was an incident of betrayal the even predates that first relationship — maybe something from your family of origin, or a relationship from your youth. Whatever it was, you were still walking around with negative energy within you, and it was time for the energy to come out.

The universe has a funny way of helping us release our pain: It gives us more pain. It presents us with an opportunity to get our hopes up, believe magic will come, and then it all comes crashing down. With that, the thin dam that was holding back the residual pain bursts, and all we can do is cry.

That's exactly what you did. You broke down and sobbed.

If you were to look at this incident from a "rational" standpoint, you'd wonder why you reacted so badly. After all, you didn't spend much time with the guy. He was a jerk pretty much from the beginning, so it's not like you had a lot invested.

So why did it hurt so badly? Because of all your old pain, the disappointment from the past that you're still carrying around. Because you so wanted a change.

Here's my advice: Roll with it. Allow yourself to feel the pain, disappointment and betrayal. Honor the experience. You're cleaning out the old wounds—and once you do, you'll be in a much better place to attract a new relationship.

As the negative emotions dissipate, replace them with joy. Notice joy wherever you can — perhaps in a lovely view, the affection of a pet, a checkout clerk who's nice to you. Then, feel gratitude for the moment of joy.

Eventually, if you keep going, the balance will shift. You'll feel less pain and more joy. And then you'll be ready for a wonderful new relationship.

I promise you, this is not a setback. It is a step in your healing.

Beginning the journey to wholeness

Last week, I posted *Letters to Lovefraud: Who we used to be,* written by the reader who posts as "Panther." She called herself a "new survivor," having just left the sociopath and gone "No Contact" less than a month ago. She wrote:

> Through reading various Lovefraud articles, I've realized that the veterans have so much invaluable advice to offer. However, at times I wonder how the voice of a survivor sounded right after the break. The reason this matters to me is because the veterans seem so much stronger than I feel right now. I cannot help but wonder, as I read through their wise words, if they have something I don't have, which enabled them to get over this.

To Panther and other Lovefraud newbies: The only difference between you and the veterans is time. We've been on the healing journey longer than you have.

I left my sociopathic ex-husband in February of 1999. That was years ago! I'll tell you what I was like when the wounds were raw. Here's what I wrote on page 287 of my book, *Love Fraud — How marriage to a sociopath fulfilled my spiritual plan.* In this part, I'm describing my state of mind, and state of being, when I discovered the treachery of my ex-husband:

> James Montgomery proclaimed his love to me — just

as he had proclaimed his love to 20 or 30 other women who had discretionary income and access to credit. I was just another pawn in a long line of women who heard the words "I love you" and believed them.

Why had this happened to me? All I ever wanted was what everyone wants — companionship, happiness, love. I was a good, considerate person. I worked hard. I treated people fairly. I did not deserve to be so exploited.

I paced up and down the hallway, my thoughts tumbling over each other, building into a mountain of pain and confusion. I leaned my back against the wall and slid to the floor, talking to myself. I felt like I should cry, but I could not. My dog, Beau, worriedly licked my face.

I was angry. I was outraged. Yet all I felt was numbness. I decided to call my therapist, Elaine Anderson. Luckily, she was available to do a session with me right then, over the phone.

I lay on the bed in my spare room, the meditation room, and told Elaine what I had found in James' papers: Correspondence to his business associates that was full of lies. Letters from women asking for their money back. Stock certificates made out to many of these women. Proof that the corporation issuing the stock certificates was defunct.

The dam within me began to crack, and then it burst. I cried. I groaned. I choked. Emotional pain rose from deep within me to the surface of my awareness, like pus rising from a deep infection. Painful energy traveled to various parts of my body — my hands, my eyes, my heart. My hands clenched. I struggled to breathe.

I don't know how long it went on. But slowly, the pain dissipated.

That was the beginning of my journey to recovery. I spent many, many hours curled up on the floor, crying. I also spent many hours envisioning my ex-husband's face on a pillow and pounding it with my fists, pounding until I collapsed. I spent many hours with my therapist, coaxing the anger and bitterness out of my emotions and out of my soul.

The betrayal of the sociopath creates deep, deep pools of pain and disappointment within us. To recover and regain ourselves, we have to drain those pools. It takes time.

And then, as we drain them, we find more pain and disappointment in the pools, left over from injuries that we experienced before the sociopath. In fact, it was those injuries that made us vulnerable to the sociopath in the first place. Those emotions must also be drained.

Healing doesn't just happen — we have to make a conscious decision to face all of the negativity head on. If we don't make the decision to heal, if we just try to put the experience of the sociopath behind us without dealing with the pain — well, then it was all a waste, we didn't learn anything, and we're likely to repeat it by finding another sociopath.

Recovery is possible, but it takes time and commitment. Here the words I said to myself time and time again: "Just keep going."

So to all of you who are just starting out, just keep going. I promise you, you can overcome, you can recover, and you can find peace.

Recovering from a sociopathic relationship is different

A Lovefraud reader asked me what I thought of advice offered on a website called "Womensdivorce.com." In a post about relationships after divorce, the website says women should start dating as soon as possible. It also seems to advocate that women engage in brief sexual affairs, and find a transitional partner who can help a woman heal, but whom she shouldn't marry.

My reaction is that this advice may be okay for someone involved in one of those amicable divorces, where the partners simply grew apart, are still on speaking terms or even friends, and want what is best for their children. The advice is terrible for someone who has been heavily damaged by marriage to a sociopath.

People who have endured marriage to a sociopath need time — perhaps a lot of time — to rebuild themselves. Healing may have two distinct dimensions.

Recovering from the sociopathic relationship

First, you need to recover from the sociopathic relationship. The difficulty of the recovery depends on the psychological damage done.

I now know that I was relatively lucky in the type of predator that found me, although it sure didn't seem that way at the time. My ex-husband, James Montgomery, only wanted my money. He lied to me, he used me, he betrayed me — but he didn't try to destroy me. When my money was gone, he just abandoned me.

Many Lovefraud readers had experiences that were far worse

than mine. Some of you endured physical and sexual violence, gaslighting, threats and brainwashing. Some of you continue to suffer because you have children with the sociopath, and your ex purposely tries to use the children to hurt you.

If you are raw from one of these extremely damaging relationships, the last thing you should do is try to find a new partner. Instead, you need to focus on personal healing.

The first step is to take care of yourself physically — eat well, find time for exercise, avoid drugs and alcohol, get enough sleep. You also need to rebuild emotionally. There are two different paths of emotional recovery. One is allowing yourself to grieve, and feel the anger and pain. The other is finding ways to bring joy into your life, however small. Nourishing encounters with friends and family whom you can trust will help.

People often ask, how long should it take to recover? There is no standard answer to this question. Recovery takes as long as it takes. But until you are feeling stronger and healthier, it is best not to get involved in another romance.

Here's an important reason why: Sociopaths target vulnerable people. If you are not yet healed, you are vulnerable, and a prime target for another sociopath.

Recovering from deeper injury

Many Lovefraud readers, as you make your way through recovery, have realized that the marriage to a sociopath was not the first damaging relationship in your life. There was an older, deeper injury that made you susceptible to the sociopath in the first place.

Some of you recognize that a previous romantic relationship was exploitative. Some of you realize that one or both of your parents were disordered. For you, the games sociopaths play may have seemed normal, because that's what you grew up with.

The pain caused by the most recent partner may cause you to realize that you have a long history of mistreatment. In fact, sometimes recognizing trauma in your past helps clear up one of the big mysteries of involvement with a sociopath. It answers the question, "Why did I allow this predator into my life?"

There may even be spiritual reasons for the dangerous encounter, which I talk about in my book, *Love Fraud—How marriage to a sociopath fulfilled my spiritual plan.* So before looking for love again, you need to recover from the sociopath, and you need to recover from any deeper traumas as well. Thankfully, you can do both at once. The process is the same as described above — slow physical and emotional healing.

So as you walk the road to recovery, be careful about listening to advice from others. As we well know, most people have no clue about what it's like to be involved with a sociopath. They have not walked in your shoes, so however well meant, their suggestions may not be helpful or healthy for you.

The first step in recovering from a sociopath: staying alive

Lovefraud received the following email from a reader whom we'll call "Lillian."

> Yes. It happened to me. It took him six years but he left. He left me holding two mortgages in both our names. He left me once I ran out of cash. He left me when I got laid off. I am almost 50 years old and I have nothing. I haven't heard from him in over a year. He encouraged me to buy a bigger, more expensive house than I would have on my own and came up with half the down. He moved in. Wouldn't pay anything. Got us a joint account and credit card. I worked. He didn't even buy groceries. He bought himself a boat after three years of hell as I got angrier and angrier because he just lay on the couch. Then he sailed to Mexico and didn't come back. His rich widow of a prominent heart surgeon called me one day. He had told her he owned property up here and that he had ended a relationship — which he hadn't. He got really angry then and cleaned out the joint account of my funds, of course, since there was never any joint about it. He lives in Mexico on his boat and has a house in Oakland. She feels like Cinderella right now and thinks I am the evil stepsister.
>
> I had $400K in cash. No revolving debt. Two retirement accounts and supported my husband and kids. Well fast forward. I have no cash. No retirement accounts.

$70K in revolving debt and no job. I am ruined. I am so traumatized and messed up that I can't function. I just cry. I reach out and no one is there. I am extremely isolated. I want to die. He is living in Mexico and suing me for half the house. He isn't done with me yet. And I am just two months away from living in a tent. No one cares. No one understands. Everyone thinks that somehow I either deserve this and or it's my fault. I am done for. I don't know that I can be helped even if I knew someone who could help me. That's the story. Sad but true. I wish I were dead.

After a devastating encounter with a sociopath, the most important thing we have to do is stay alive.

We may have lost our money, our homes, our jobs, our health, our self-esteem, our hopes and our dreams, but we cannot lose our selves.

This is basic, but crucial. We cannot die.

Not everyone succeeds at this essential task. Not everyone is able to continue living in the face of monstrous personal betrayal. In these cases, the sociopath truly wins. Dr. Leedom calls it "murder by suicide."

There is an old adage, "Where there's life, there's hope." When dealing with the aftermath of a sociopath, this is the truth. A sociopath's goal is always to win, and sometimes to destroy us in the process. When we stay alive, we deny the sociopath's victory.

We can also start a process that, over time, will enable us to claim victory for ourselves.

It doesn't seem that way in the blackness of despair as we survey the wreckage of our lives. But as many of us have learned, amid the wreckage we may discover that our broken ideas and beliefs actually needed to be broken and thrown away. We were operating under false conceptions of ourselves, conceptions that made us vulnerable to the predators.

We learn that if we stay alive, we can begin to rebuild our lives, and when we do, we will be living our own truth.

So how do we do it? We keep putting one foot in front of the other. We cry when we need to, then we pick ourselves up and push on. We keep going forward, even though we don't believe we can.

The road to recovery takes time and patience. It takes recognizing that we may be suffering from post-traumatic stress disorder (PSTD). It takes caring about ourselves and being kind to ourselves.

The first step is staying alive.

Please, Lillian, we know your situation is very, very bad. But don't let him win.

Find meaning in the betrayal

Lovefraud received the following email from a reader who posts as "lostgirl."

I fell hopelessly in love with (read as I would have given him my real heart and died for him) a sociopath /psychopath.

Skip the details.

I am four years divorced.

There isn't a day that goes by that I don't grieve the loss of the relationship I thought I had. I cognitively know that the person I married was not who I thought he was and I even believe I know how he came to be. Unfortunately, I have never felt anger, only sadness for what I viewed as the person he could have been that was taken from him long ago. I see him as an addict and myself as having been addicted to him.

Somehow, now, I still cannot move on. I have been through many short relationships, all ended — well for me — and usually I ended the relationship when I noticed red flags, the ones I kept close at heart. Again, I am in a new relationship and experiencing all the anxiety all over again (each new relationship triggers this). Including nightmares of the ex-sociopath and agonizing over how to know when someone is genuine. Good words are empty and promises of future fall on my deaf ears because I was disheartened so gravely before.

I have become cold and detached. I feel less emotion for every single thing in my life than at any time ever. All things I own, animals, family, I feel as though I am in a stage of suspended life, I cannot bond. I take care of my animals, I take care of my parents, nothing I own feels as if it's mine, only borrowed, including relationships. I feel fake and alone.

I truly liked the person I met that I am in a relationship with now, but as with all the others after a short time (three months), I begin to feel less and look critically at their words and life — as if I am subconsciously talking myself out of taking the risk of succeeding because of the pool of "thought I had's" that live inside my head.

I know that a good relationship takes time to grow. How can I give myself the time to grow a relationship when I am so busy still flashing back to a relationship that was agony? He compliments me and I toss it aside. He talks about his life and experiences and I'm trying to assemble timeframes in my head to make sure he isn't lying to me. It's as if I'm trying to analyze my way in to a sincere relationship by slicing and dicing all the input/information I'm given. In the meantime I've dehumanized the relationship in my head and nearly severed any chance at bonding.

I have read post after post from people and articles all over the internet. What I haven't found is any truly helpful advice for someone like me.

I fear I have lost the ability to connect permanently because I cannot logically define what is not deceitful at the moment it occurs. What is unselfish, I look for selfishness in. All good is lost because I have become obsessed with what is wrong with what is right.

How do I get back to identifying reality and trusting when it is proper? I feel that my mind was raped and I have lost the ability to connect on any level with anyone. I feel like a shell and I can see through everyone in my life, it would be so easy to be just like him (the ex) but I am not driven to "want" like he did. I see the holes in people and it is so easy for me to identify what is exploitable.

I hate this person I've become. I want to climb out of the shell and return to who I was before I fell in "love."

Help I'm lost.

Realm of Numb

A very wise spiritual counselor once said that unresolved anger becomes rage, and unresolved rage becomes numbness. I think that's what has happened to Lostgirl—she has moved into the Realm of Numb.

She was so in love with the sociopath that she would have died for him. In effect, that is what she did. Her life spark is gone. She no longer finds joy in her family and animals. She looks for deception in new relationships. She no longer trusts herself to know when she can trust another human being.

The Realm of Numb isn't a place of pain. It's a place of emptiness, of nothingness, of void. And it's a place where none of us should be.

But how do we escape? How do we leave behind the feeling of fakeness, and recover the feeling of authenticity?

Search for meaning

One of the books that Lovefraud recommends to everyone who has experienced the trauma of a sociopath is *The Betrayal Bond,* by Patrick J. Carnes, Ph.D. The book explains the circumstances that can cause us to form traumatic bonds with an abuser, and provides exercises to help readers unravel those bonds.

When I read the book, I highlighted only one sentence that Carnes wrote, and this is it:

> My experience with survivors of trauma is that every journey of recovery depends on the survivor coming to a point where all that person has gone through means something.

This is the key. This is how we truly recover. There is always meaning in what has happened to us, although it can be difficult to find. In fact, that's what makes the destructive relationships with sociopaths so excruciatingly painful — we can't figure out why they happened. We did nothing to deserve the betrayal. Our intentions were honorable. So why did this happen to us?

Answers in the past

For many of us, the answer lies in our past. If we've experienced an abusive relationship, and were not able to recover, we are primed for another abusive relationship. The problem is even more insidious if we were abused as children, because our whole idea of what is "normal" in a relationship is terribly skewed.

But issues of the past need not be as overtly damaging as abuse. Perhaps our childhoods were basically okay, but we've always felt somewhat insignificant, or undeserving of love. We may have had "good enough" parenting, but our parents focused on achievement, and we grew up believing that we were loved for what we could do, not for who we are. Beliefs like these, even when they're unconscious, can create vulnerabilities for sociopaths to exploit.

It's also possible that there is a deep spiritual reason for becoming involved with a sociopath. This is what happened to me. I believe that we all come into this life with lessons to learn, and sometimes the lessons are painful.

Some people may not be comfortable with the idea of searching for the meaning of the entanglement with a sociopath. It may feel easier to think we were just in the wrong place at the wrong time, and ran into the wrong person. We just want to brush the encounter aside.

I think this attitude is only a band-aid, and sooner or later, if we don't find the root cause, we'll repeat the experience. There is meaning, and discovering it leads to healing.

Research, therapy, introspection

So how do we do this? How do we find meaning in what may appear to be a random victimization?

Here's an important point: True healing doesn't just happen by itself. True healing requires personal effort.

The first step is to be willing to look for the meaning. Sometimes this, in itself, is difficult. We may be afraid of the painful memories. We may have tried to shove the experience into the past. We may be afraid that if we start crying, we'll never stop. By being willing, we face these fears, and we may discover, to our surprise, that we can overcome them.

The actual process of finding meaning will probably involve some combination of research, therapy and introspection.

Research: This means educating ourselves not only about the sociopathic disorder, but also about the characteristics and attitudes of a whole, healthy person. We need to understand what we've been through, and what we want to become.

Therapy: By therapy, I mean seeking support from other human beings. This could mean working with a therapist or counselor. Or, it may simply be seeking the advice of an understanding, trusted friend, or other members of Lovefraud.

Introspection: Somewhere, deep within us, we know the answers. If we can quiet our minds, with meditation or just sitting in stillness, information will bubble up into our awareness. We may become aware of the mistaken, limiting beliefs that we didn't know we had. We may receive intuitive guidance about what we should do. If we allow ourselves to seek the truth within, we will find it.

Emotional experience

We cannot expect the process of finding meaning to be simply an intellectual exercise. The bottom line is, we are in pain, pain that may be so entrenched that it has become numbness.

Pain is emotional. The release of pain is also emotional. Therefore, the search for meaning is an emotional experience. The meaning may be buried under anger, hatred, disappointment and fear, and we need to plow through all those emotions in order to find it. And this isn't a one-time event. We may release anger, only to find more rise up to take its place. This may happen again, and again, and again. The truth is, we are all walking around in pools of pain, and draining the pools takes time.

The expression of these emotions is not pretty, and many people may not have the strength to be with us as we do it. I found that I could only do it with my therapist, or alone. So I sat in my spare room, which I call the meditation room, crying, pounding pillows in rage, and recording my rants in my journal.

But once we release the emotions, they're gone, leaving room within us to fill with other emotions—like hope, love and joy.

To Lostgirl

Lostgirl, here is what I want you to know: You were betrayed by a sociopath. This is an experience that happened to you. It is not who you are. You are you; the experience is the experience. Do not confuse the two.

There is a meaning for the experience, and it will help you to discover it. This will require effort and commitment on your part. Take the steps. Make a commitment to yourself, to your own growth and happiness. What better commitment could you make?

Find the meaning. But don't go on a self-help expedition to the exclusion of all else. Here's a secret: When you focus on any joy in your life, no matter how small, and feel gratitude for the joy, you create an internal energy that attracts more joy.

Healing our hearts is always the answer. To heal, unearth the pain, and replace it with joy. The process may take time, but eventually the life spark will return, brighter than it ever was.

When to trust your man (or woman)

The question was, "When can you trust your man?" A reporter who was writing an article on the topic for a major women's magazine asked the question. It showed up in my email because I subscribe to a service that distributes questions from reporters to experts all around the world who may be able to answer them.

I knew what the reporter was looking for. She wanted succinct little tips like:

- "You can trust your man if he always shows up when he says he will, or at least calls to tell you he'll be late."
- "You can trust your man if he introduces you to his mother."
- "You can trust your man if he shows you his income tax return."

But, after being married to a sociopath, and hearing the stories of so many Lovefraud readers, I knew that these external signs may not be accurate.

The luring stage

In the beginning of a relationship, the luring stage, sociopaths can be reliable and punctual. They may seem proud to introduce you to their families. They may appear to be financially solvent.

Sociopathic individuals can appear to be deserving of respect, love and trust as long as it suits their purpose. These predators know what they are supposed to do to win over a lover. And they are capable of actually doing it — at least until they feel like they no longer need to.

Once they have their hooks set in you, they may be late — or even disappear for days or weeks with no explanation. Their families may trip over themselves to be good to you — probably because they want you to take the parasite off their hands. And they may flash cash and financial documents — cash taken from the previous partner, and documents that are forged.

So how do you know when to trust your man — or woman? Here's my answer: You can trust your partner when you can trust yourself.

Trusting yourself

When it comes to romantic relationships, there are two dimensions to trusting yourself.

The first is your own sense of self. You know who you are, what you want, and where your boundaries are. You know that you deserve to be loved simply for being yourself. You understand that a relationship involves giving and taking by both parties, not one person doing all the giving and the other all the taking. You will not jeopardize your well-being in order to have companionship.

The second dimension is trusting your intuition. Your gut, your body, your sixth sense, will tell you when something is wrong. You must have enough faith in yourself that you can hear or feel the intuitive messages, and pay attention to them. We get in trouble when we allow ourselves to be talked out of what our intuition is telling us. When a person or suggestion makes us feel uncomfortable, that's our early warning system, and we must trust ourselves enough to listen.

I responded to the magazine reporter's inquiry. I told her than the time to trust a man is when we trust ourselves. She didn't reply. I assume that my answer wasn't what she wanted.

10 tips to start dating again after the sociopath

Editor's note: The Lovefraud reader who writes as "Glinda" sent the following letter. I'll provide my thoughts at the end of her letter.

"NEVER Dating Again" Punishment or Prudence?

I have most of my life back in order, post sociopath. Work is good; I have friends; I have hobbies; and my kids are wellcared for and seem to be well adjusted to our family routine. I also don't worry and think about getting asked out much. I'm pretty sure I put a "nuh uh" sign out, in neon. I haven't had any interest in dating — in fact, I've sworn off relationships in general. I'm not lonely. I've filled my life and don't feel empty or sad. I have a terrible track record in picking men — and a worse record in the ones who have chosen me.

On the occasion I do go out, it's the resident bar fly loser that comes to talk to me. I don't even have to dress suggestively — I can wear a blouse I wore to the office and dress pants and be among women who are dressed "out on the prowl" and loser-boy finds ME. It seems safer not to date, obviously. Admittedly, ONCE in awhile, I think, "It would be nice to have someone in my life." The feeling hasn't been strong enough to act on it. The other day, I ordered a cheap wedding band looking ring to wear when I go out, in hopes that it will be a deterrent.

Recently I joined a hallway conversation at work with a couple of people I've known and worked with for years, and another guy I had seen around, but didn't know. I interjected funny things into the conversation — my MO really — humor. I have a dry and sarcastic sense of humor without much fear of looking silly. I'm not terribly self-conscious these days. I don't worry about men at the office being interested in me — I'm not looking and decent guys never ask. For the most part, it never crosses my mind. At home, I joke about now being A-sexual. "New" guy is laughing at my jokes and sending furtive glances my way. I notice, but don't think much of it. I recently dropped some weight and I'm getting noticed again. I still have a ways to go, but he isn't the first guy to give me a second look lately.

A day or so goes by, and I have a Facebook friend request from him. Hmm. I am friends with several folks from work. I think about it for a couple of days — I don't know him that well. But, we don't work on a project together and we're not under the same leadership tree. I don't do stupid, drunken antics and then also post the pics on FB. I don't complain about work or other coworkers on FB either, decide it is "safe enough" to friend him.

Next day, he comments on something of mine. Hmm. That feeling that he liked what he saw/heard gets a little stronger — Maybe he just thinks I'm funny. I pawn it off on that.

Later, I get a FB msg. Hmm. Not entirely odd — I get frequent msgs on FB — but —? We chat on FB, back and forth, 2 or 3 msgs a day. Nothing overwhelming, very banal conversation. But the fact that it's starting to build up makes me think. Makes me think what? I don't know exactly. I respond to msgs, at my leisure, waiting and watching to see where this is headed. I'm being "hit on!" Ha ha! I'm not getting a creep vibe off of him — but I really don't know him. I'm nervous, but also pleased.

A few more days of FB msgs, and him hinting around but not directly asking, he asks if I'll go to lunch with him. RED ALERT!!! RED ALERT!!!! I am officially freaked out! WHY would he ask me out? Do I still have, "Easy Pickin's" stamped on my forehead? Or is he genuinely interested – and HOW THE HECK DO *I* TELL THE DIFFERENCE?????????

I should probably state here that I don't NOT want to go. I want to. That scares me as much as his asking. What happened to "no dating, ever?" It HAS been 4+ years, after all. Is it possible that I'm done "licking my wounds" and AM ready to move on – I just needed some sort of prompting? Or am I NUTS? I honestly do not know. Sigh.

I decide to accept the lunch invitation. What's the worst that can happen, right? Hahahah — I know EXACTLY what the worst that can happen includes. I fret over my decision for a couple of days—trying to separate if I'm getting a bad vibe from him or if one of my baggage U-hauls has dumped the contents on my front lawn.

I have refreshed myself on the red flags on LoveFraud. I've reread Martha Stout's "Rule of Threes." So far, in our FB and emails, he doesn't match up with any of those. He appears to have some qualities I prefer. Also, he's employed, just bought a new car so he should have some credit — and the car isn't over the top. It's in the range of what most of us buy in our salary range.

We've talked a few times at work and I haven't noticed anything out of the ordinary — and believe me, I'm LOOKING for it. I've been looking for ANY indication that my bad man magnet is still operational — any excuse to nip this in the bud and go back to my comfort zone. I ask LOTS of questions — how else do you get to know someone but asking, right? I've asked him about things he likes and doesn't like — without already having my likes and dislikes as ready answers. (I'm a little smarter than I used to be.) He gets a little tongue-tied when talking to me (a good sociopath never gets tongue tied). It's kinda cute, really — as long as it's sincere and not some new "game" he figured out.

SLOW SLOW SLOW. I'm in no hurry as this plays out. I've spent some time on the Internet — yes, I Googled him. The alma mater he lists on his profile actually matches the hit I got for his graduation (with honors). He hasn't mentioned it — it's the only "hit" I got. We've talked on the phone a couple of times; it was nice. The more we talk, the more I feel a bit more at ease. Not glib. Not a braggart. Not pushy. (I HATE PUSHY!) Not exciting, and you know what I mean — just normal-ish.

I'm still suspicious — well, let's call it cautious and reserved, shall we? I went to a male coworker (and friend) that I trust. We've worked together a long, long time—I could trust him with any secret. He also knows what I went through with the spath. I pulled him aside and asked him if I still had "Victim Here" written all over me, or if I was "dateable"? Seriously. *I* think I've changed. *I* think I've grown wiser. I LIKE to think that — but do we really know until we test that theory? After he rolled his eyes and I reminded him of where I've been, I got the "dateable" answer. Ha ha!

In addition to Googling him, I've tried to gain some insight on my conflicting thoughts. I've tried searching "Dating After Sociopath." I got a whole lot of nothing. There are tons of sites that discuss escaping and recovering from a spath (which is good and unfortunately necessary) — but what about the next step? HOW does one take the next step without feeling crazy again?

It's not just "Dating After Divorce." I didn't just "lose interest" or "grow apart" from my spouse — or even "just" get dumped — I all but got my soul sucked out. In a couple of weeks, I lost my husband, my imaginary life, my home, and everything, EVERYTHING I thought I knew. He'd also been sexually abusing my child. For years — while every day telling me how much he loved me. For months, I kept discovering more and more betrayals and lies. How on God's green earth do you EVER believe a SINGLE word again? How do you trust another's motivation again? HOW? The vast majority of people in my life are those whom I've known for a decade — or 2 or 3. How do you "vet" a new person? And do I, or my kids, deserve my taking that risk? After everything that happened, everything I allowed to happen, by putting up with nonsense, shouldn't I stay single/solo? Shouldn't that be my punishment?

I'm still talking to "new" guy. If he is sincere — he's probably feeling a bit perplexed. I answer many questions with a question and frequently give vague answers — I'm not drawing anyone a freaking roadmap to destroy my soul again. What he sees is probably my blowing hot and cold. A more accurate description would be just guarded and REALLY guarded.

Our lunch out is Tuesday. I'm not sure whether to say good luck to me — or him.

Donna Andersen replies

We are allowed to recover from the trauma of the sociopathic relationship. We are allowed to move on. In fact, if we don't move on, if we don't take our lives back, we are still in the trauma. It is healthy to put an end to it.

Recently a reporter was writing an article and sent out a query: "How do you know when to trust 'your man'?" I believe the answer is you can trust your man (or woman) when you can trust yourself.

Of course, that is exactly what Glinda is struggling with — as are many of us who had multiple run-ins with sociopaths and other bad actors. How do you know that you're no longer sending out the "I'm a victim" vibes?

For Glinda, I believe the answer is in the beginning of her letter. She is basically at peace. Work, friends, hobbies and kids are all good. She's not lonely, empty or sad. All of this means that she is not looking for fulfillment from outside of herself. She is balanced and centered, and this is the best place from which to start dating.

We get in trouble when we feel that we are not enough on our own, and we need another person in order for us to feel successful, validated or complete. It's the desperation vibe, the neediness vibe, the incompleteness vibe, which attracts the predators. If we're in a place where companionship would be a pleasant addition to our already reasonably okay lives, then we're in a place where we can invite someone to join us.

This is really the biggest sign that we're ready to move on. But here are a few other tips to keep in mind.

Dating tips

1. Know the warning signs of sociopathic behavior in dating situations. Keep in mind, however, that you may not see these behaviors right away. Sociopaths can successfully put on an act for quite a long time. Read my book, *Red Flags of Love Fraud — 10 signs you're dating a sociopath.*

2. If you ever see a behavior that makes you respond, "Huh? What was that about?" — pay attention. It may be a sign that the mask has slipped, just enough for you to catch a glimpse of what is really there.

3. Check the person out. It is now commonplace for people to Google potential partners right away, so don't feel like you're out of line by doing it. In fact, Google creatively. Check out the person's name, employment and any background information that he or she offers you.

4. Do not allow most of your relationship to be email, text or even phone. Experts estimate that 65% to 90% of the meaning in communication comes from nonverbal cues. With email, text and phone, these cues are missing, so we don't get the full range of human communications. So what do we do? We fill in the gaps with what we want to believe. We fall in love with our own fantasies.

5. Avoid long-distance relationships. You want to be able to get together with this person easily, and, if it works out, frequently. You want to be able to meet friends and family, see his or her workplace, and spend time together in a variety of environments. If you can't conveniently drive to get together, the relation-

ship is probably a bad idea.

6. Do not throw away a perception. If some behavior or statement strikes you as odd or troublesome, do not let the person talk you out of it or explain it away. Do not let the person gaslight you into believing it never happened.

7. Consider what your friends and family say. If people are telling you that the guy or gal is bad news, they have a bad feeling, or any other negative feedback, at least listen. You may even have to solicit their opinions. Often people have reservations, but they don't want to spoil your happiness, so they don't say anything. Give people an opportunity to speak. However, if you have bad vibes, and your friends and family say you should give the person a chance, trust yourself.

8. Go slow.

9. Trust your instincts. We all have an internal warning system. If your stomach goes in knots, the hair on the back of your neck rises, or you feel fear, listen to yourself. Many of us felt the warnings before we became involved with sociopaths — the feeling that something wasn't right — but we didn't pay attention. Your body will tell you when someone should be avoided.

10. The first person you go out with may not be the love of your life, and that's okay. Sometimes people come into our lives to help us continue to heal. You may have a few interim involvements before you find a person who has the potential to be a permanent partner.

It is possible to recover, to heal, to fall in love again. And I can tell you, the love I have with my husband now is richer and more fulfilling than anything I experienced before the sociopath.

Glinda, it sounds to me like you're in a good place and you can trust yourself. There are plenty of good, empathetic and loving people out there. Don't feel like you need to know how it will all turn out before you start. Let everything evolve, and pay attention to what you experience, and what you feel, all along the way.

Letter to Lovefraud: I wanted him to be the guy of my dreams, but he's nothing but a fraud

Editor's note: Lovefraud received this email from a reader whom we'll call "Loralei." At the end of her email, I'll comment on it.

When I was young, I was emotionally and physically abused by my mother. She didn't give me any black eyes, but I did get slapped, my hair pulled, and it was clear that the world revolved around my mother. I lived in fear, and when I wasn't the target of her anger, I was ignored.

Fast forward 40 years. I am a successful business-woman, I live in a nice Chicago suburb, I have friends, I like to help people, and I was tired of not having a love life. For some goofy reason, I posted an ad on Craigslist; I met a really handsome guy named Robert. He said he was a banker, he also said he just got back from Iraq (that he was in the army), he was well dressed, he said he was "going through" a divorce, and he seemed articulate, and nice. We quickly moved into a sexual relationship.

I noticed some odd things. His communication was primarily email or text messages. It was extremely abrupt — no mention of feelings — just very minimal, concise, fact-based conversations. And he was a white collar professional (a banker), but he said he just got back from Iraq? He didn't have a buzz haircut, and he didn't look terribly in shape.

Checking him out

While I thought I struck the goldmine, an inner voice told me I should check things out. I found that he didn't live in the town that he said he lived in. I found that he wasn't "going through" a divorce, but in fact he was already divorced. And I wrote to the military, and found out, yes, he was in the Army, but that was 20 years ago when he was a college student, and he was NEVER in Iraq.

Over the course of weeks and months I learned more. He actually lived in the same home with his ex-wife and their children.

Then he took a business trip, and he told me he took an extra day or two to go to West Point to visit his Army friends (well, of course I knew he never went to West Point) so I snooped and I found that he went to stay for a weekend at a romantic bed and breakfast with another woman. He took other business trips. I was suspicious, and I placed ads on Craigslist under the romantic encounter section in the city he was visiting. Sure enough, he was replying to those ads trying to stir up a one-night stand. Both times I was crushed, I told him straight up he was busted.

Kept falling for him

Yet, stupidly, over the course of weeks and months, I kept falling for this guy. He texted me every morning, "GM," and every night, "GN," we emailed and texted all day, we laughed, we flirted. We saw each other periodically, and he was attentive, and kind, and fun, and complimented me and held my hand, and was unfailingly polite. The visits were always during business hours. Why would that be, if he was divorced?

I confronted him with lie after lie. Some he acknowledged, some he ignored. The lies continued, along with the continued flirting, continued sex. I was baffled. I cried all the time. We would have incredible sex, it lasted 4 - 6- 8 hours and then there would be nothing for a whole month. I felt abused. I would tell him how I felt, he said he loved me, but nothing in his behavior changed. He would show no empathy at all. A woman called my home looking for him once — she said they had made plans to meet, and she wondered where he was. I didn't understand. At one point I was so desperate I reached out to his ex-wife. I asked her if she was still sleeping with him. Her voice got really meek and scared-like, and she said she wasn't sleeping with him. I thought it was really weird. But it told me she obviously knew about everything, and wanted to bury her head in the sand.

Couldn't leave him

I tried to break up with him in May of 2009. I cried again. He was distressed. He said he knew he was shallow, he knew he was selfish, and he wanted me to stay. I felt bad, couldn't leave him. We went back and forth and back and forth for about a year. I would leave him, then he would text me and make me pity him, and I'd go back. Then he would ignore me, and then, before I knew it, we'd be back together again.

It was a very addictive relationship. That fall he introduced me to a bunch of his colleagues as his "wife." And he took me on a trip to Seattle on a train, and whispered in my ear how everybody could clearly see how in love we were. Were we in love? How could that be, if he spends every night and every weekend with his ex-wife? He said it was his favorite daydream to imagine me being his wife.

I couldn't understand it. How could a nice, polite, educated man lie to me? So I read books. I read about avoidant personality disorder. I read about psychopathy, antisocial personality disorder, I read about anxiety disorders, I must have read 25 psych books. I read, "When your lover is a liar" and every other book out there.

So do I believe his words? They're inconsistent. Do I believe his actions? They're inconsistent too.

I began therapy, and I began to see how the way he was treating me was similar to the way my mother treated me. I invited the abuse on myself, apparently repeating a cycle I learned in childhood. Somehow I got strong enough to finally push away from him. The first few weeks I felt like I was going to die. Every day I think about him, and nearly every day I feel rage, I feel raped. I can't believe I kept making excuses for him. I can't believe I got sucked into this fantasy. I wanted him to be the guy of my dreams, but he's nothing but a fraud. A love fraud.

My comments: This is a classic Lovefraud story

Loralei's story has every typical element of a sociopathic relationship. It is a classic Lovefraud story.

First of all, Loralei was abused by her mother. Anyone who has abuse in their history is susceptible to more abuse. The traumatic bonding that takes place during these relationships makes the dynamic of abuse feel normal.

Loralei, I strongly recommend that you read *The Betrayal Bond,* by Patrick J. Carnes, Ph.D. It explains how abusive relationships affect you, and why it can be difficult to leave them.

Secondly, Loralei's intuition was working. "An inner voice told me I should check things out," she wrote. So she did. And she found out that the guy was lying to her. But she continued to see him anyway.

Why? Because Loralei was already addicted to the relationship.

Relationships with sociopaths are highly addictive. The relationships cause psychological and chemical changes in the brain that make victims feel bonded to the sociopath.

This is especially true when sex is involved. Sex enhances the natural human bonding process — it's nature's way of keeping people together to care for children. It doesn't seem to affect sociopaths — sociopaths are famous for their callous promiscuity. But partners of sociopaths, who feel normal bonding, become attached. That's why Loralei couldn't leave him.

So how can Loralei get out of a relationship with a sociopath? She must treat it as the addiction that it is. She must cut off all contact with the guy, cold turkey. No emails. No texts. No phone calls. And certainly no get-togethers. Loralei must take it one day at a time. Get through today. Then tomorrow. Then the next day.

If Loralei gives in to her addiction and has contact with him, it will be like a medical relapse, and she'll have to start all over again. But if she can maintain no contact, each day she'll get stronger, and his hold on her will be less.

But here's the most important part of this classic Lovefraud story. As awful as this relationship was, it has a nugget of gold in it. This lying, cheating abuser has brought to the surface Loralei's original emotional wound — the abuse of her mother. Now, she has the opportunity to process and let go of that deep, awful pain.

Loralei, look at the gift of this situation. Give yourself time and permission to heal. You can do it. And eventually, if you want, you'll be able to attract a healthy, satisfying relationship.

After the sociopath, advice for heartbreak

I subscribe to a service through which reporters who are looking for information for their stories can find sources. Not long ago, a reporter posted the following query:

> A reporter at a national publication is writing about the hell of heartbreak and is looking for people to interview who have experienced a romantic breakup or divorce and who have creative/unusual advice on how to get through the day-to-day emotional turmoil of it. If you've been through a breakup (as an adult), how did you deal with the emotional pain, especially in the very beginning? How did you distract yourself from your heartache? How did you keep yourself from calling or texting your former beloved? What advice would you give to someone else in the middle of a heartbreak?

Most of us are here on Lovefraud because we experienced the most devastating, heartrending breakups of all—those involving sociopaths.

Ours were not run-of-the-mill relationships where the ending was, "he's just not into you." Ours were not situations in which two people "just grew apart." Ours were false relationships from the very beginning, in which we were targeted, exploited and betrayed.

Advice? Yes, I have advice

First of all, if you were involved with a sociopath, NORMAL

ADVICE DOESN'T WORK. Even though self-help gurus have sold millions of books, and even if your friends have been through many, many relationships, unless they, too, have been targeted by sociopaths, THEY DON'T KNOW WHAT THEY'RE TALKING ABOUT.

So, the first bit of advice is DON'T LISTEN TO PEOPLE WHO DON'T GET IT.

Back to positive advice. What is the one thing you need to understand if you've been involved with a sociopath? IT'S NOT YOU!

Oh, the sociopath certainly told you that you were the problem, told you that you had problems, and even blamed you for his or her atrocious behavior. But that was all part of the manipulation. Sociopaths intentionally make you doubt yourself. Sometimes it's to make you malleable so they can take advantage of you; sometimes it's just for their own entertainment. If you're feeling nuts, you are having a rational reaction to an insane situation, and your ex is the one causing the insanity.

Next you need to know that the relationship NEVER WOULD HAVE WORKED. Although sociopaths lavishly proclaim their love, they're lying. Sociopaths are incapable of love. But they have learned that if they mouth the words "I love you," they can get what they want. And what they want is to exploit you.

If you've been involved with someone like this, there is nothing you could have done differently. Nothing would have made the situation better. The sociopath cannot be satisfied, and cannot change.

So how should you view your experience? DON'T TAKE IT PERSONALLY. Yes, really. The fact that you were mistreated had nothing to do with you or your behavior. It had everything to do with the fact that you were involved with a cruel, heartless sociopath.

If your ex didn't do it to you, he or she would have done it to someone else. Why? Because that's what they do.

Finally, YOU CAN RECOVER, BUT IT WILL TAKE TIME. This is not a normal breakup. It wasn't only your heart that was broken. It was also your view of the world.

Give yourself time and permission to heal. Surround yourself with people who truly care about you, and embark on a program of NO CONTACT with the sociopath. Even though you pine for the individual, understand that you fell in love with a mirage, and what you're feeling is residual addiction to the relationship.

Do not call. Do not text. Do not send email. The stronger your commitment to NO CONTACT, the faster you will mend.

Take positive steps. Find joy and happiness anywhere you can, and let them seep into the empty hole that was your heart. Eventually, your heart will fill up and you can try again—with much more wisdom than you had before.

Why you feel so shattered by the sociopath's betrayal

When you first begin to realize that you've been involved with a sociopath, you may feel unhinged, like you've lost your bearings in the world and you're drifting.

"How can someone who claims to love me be so cruel?"

"Do you mean he (she) never loved me? It was all a lie?"

"I never knew people like this existed!"

You've had your heart broken before, but no previous relationship compared to this. Even if you've managed to get away from this toxic person, you feel lost. Your well-meaning friends and family are urging you to get over it, to put it behind you, but you can't.

Why? Why is it so difficult to overcome the sociopathic experience?

I believe it's because nobody talks about the fact that sociopaths live among us. It's a giant, malevolent skeleton in humanity's closet.

Society's myths

All our lives, society bombards us with messages such as "everybody is basically the same," "all men are created equal," "we all just want to be loved," and "there's good in everyone."

We strive to follow the Golden Rule — "Treat others the way you want to be treated" — believing that if we're good to people, they'll be good to us in return.

As much as we would like these ideas to be universal, they are not. But no cultural institutions, such as schools, churches, or even women's magazines, tells us that there are exceptions to all these truisms.

No one tells us that criminals and terrorists aren't the only bad people in the world. No one tells us that our neighbors, co-workers, or fellow church members, who look just like us, may, in fact, be human predators.

So when we run into these human predators, we are totally unprepared.

The big contradiction

We don't know about sociopaths — people who live their lives by exploiting others. Professionally, they may be diagnosed as antisocial, narcissistic, borderline, histrionic or psychopathic. If you add up the official estimates for the number of people who have these personality disorders, it totals 12% to 16% of the population.

For this segment of the population, all those feel-good messages we get from society simply don't apply. These people are not the same as us. They do not just want to be loved. Deep down, there is no good inside.

Worldview

We all have a certain Weltanschauung, a word borrowed from German that means "worldview." We have ideas and beliefs about how the world works, the nature of things, and the nature of people.

After a lifetime of absorbing cultural messages such as "everyone deserves a chance" and "love can change everything," these are the lenses through which we view the world. They are also the lenses through which we approach our relationships.

Then we experience betrayal by the sociopath.

Here's why this betrayal is so devastating: It shatters our worldview. It contradicts everything we thought we knew and understood about the world and the people in it.

We learn, much to our horror, that our worldview is not accurate. There is a certain percentage of the population — the sociopaths — for whom everything we thought we knew about humanity simply does not apply.

This is why we feel unhinged. Not only our heart is broken — our understanding of life is broken.

Wisdom

Along with emotional healing, therefore, recovery requires that we change our most fundamental beliefs.

Yes, for 88% of the population, everything we always thought remains true. But for the remaining 12%, we need to accept a new reality.

Sociopaths are totally different from the rest of us. They have no ability to love. They are motivated only by power and control.

But now we know. We know that although the majority of people are good and loving, some are not.

Having learned this lesson the hard way, we can now approach the rest of our lives with the wisdom of a survivor.

Why her happy marriage did not exist

Lovefraud received the following letter from a reader about her experience with a sociopath:

I was not in a disastrous relationship with my S. Our relationship was less than three years, our marriage less than two — when he openly cheated and decided to leave me, then played games of false reconciliation, which in hindsight were so he could have two sex partners.

The short end of my question is — How do you reconcile the basically happy marriage, the illusion of a man you married, with the horrible monster he has become in trying to create turmoil in your life and use your greatest love (your child) to hurt you?

Range of behavior

One reason why it's so difficult to spot sociopaths is because they are not all the same. Sociopathy varies from person to person. You could compare it to a trait like intelligence — not all intelligent people are intelligent in the same way. Some people are smart in academics, some people have mechanical skills, some people are artistically brilliant. They are all intelligent, but intelligent in different areas of life.

Sociopathy manifests differently in different people — I like to say the disorder ranges from sleazy to serial killer. Some, therefore, are violent — but many, probably even most, are not. Some sociopaths are low-level criminals; others have successful careers in business, government, medicine, the military, education, the clergy — every possible field of endeavor.

The point is, sociopaths exhibit a range of behavior, so behavior by itself is not always a reliable way of spotting the disorder.

The mask

Sociopaths often wear a mask — until they decide that they can no longer be bothered keeping up appearances. I think that's what happened in the case of this Lovefraud reader. The sociopath she was with played the part of the committed husband — until he had enough of that game and wanted a change. Oh, he kept it going for awhile with the false reconciliation. But when he was well and truly tired of the marriage, he became the monster.

The reader didn't say how he was using the child to hurt her, but based on what I've heard from other parents, I can take a few guesses. The sociopath considers the child to be his property, and he wants to own it. Or, the sociopath thinks the child will be useful to his image — he'll be able to play the doting dad, so that he can snag another victim. Or, the sociopath simply wants to win whatever battle their custody situation has become, and win convincingly, so that our reader never has the temerity to challenge him again.

The illusion

So how does our reader reconcile the "happy marriage" with the "monster"? She has to understand that the happy marriage never existed. It was an illusion, carefully crafted by the sociopath to reel her in and get what he wanted. Once he changed his mind about what he wanted, the marriage was no longer useful to him, so he dumped it.

This is what sociopaths have in common: They are social predators. They are users. They have no heart, no conscience and no remorse. You cannot interpret them through the way you live your life. You simply have to accept the fact that they are staggeringly different from us. We feel empathy for other people. They do not.

Regardless of how it manifests, the common denominator is that these people are empty shells pretending to be human. When you look carefully inside them, you'll see nothing.

Letter to Lovefraud: I'm looking on POF, but I'm scared to move forward

Lovefraud received the following email from a reader who gives her pseudonym as "Erica."

> I've been in love with a sociopath for 5 and a half years. He lives in Portland and I live here in Vegas so that has been a great thing, however he still haunts me and I'm trying to move on so I'm enclosing a profile from an online dating site and I'd like to get your opinion of the things that he says. I'm scared to move forward because I'm scared that I'll attract another one. I seem to be surrounded by narcissism and sociopathy and I'm tired and I'm scared and I lack trust to move forward. Donna please share my email on lovefraud.com so that I can get some feedback from other members.

Erica sent a screenshot of an ad from the Plenty of Fish dating site — I assume she is considering responding to it. I'll address the ad later, but first I want to focus on the main issue of the email:

Erica, if you are scared to move forward and scared to attract another sociopath, then you are not ready to date.

Calculated seduction

Involvements with sociopaths are always emotionally and psychologically damaging, and often destructive to your finances, career, social relationships and more.

With past breakups, perhaps you suffered some heartbreak and your pride was wounded, but you were able to pick yourself up, dust yourself off, and jump back into the dating pool.

Relationships with sociopaths are not normal, so neither are the breakups.

Sociopaths engage in calculated seduction. In the beginning they love bomb you, want to be with you 24/7, make glittering promises about the future. The sex is usually unbelievable. The effect of this extraordinary attention is that you fall, and fall hard.

The attention and affection continue until the sociopath either feels that you are truly hooked, or loses interest. Then the devalue and discard begins. You were once the most important person in the world to your partner, and suddenly you are nothing. Your fall from the sociopath's pedestal is brutal, and you honestly don't know what happened.

You may think that you should be able to put the person behind you and move on as you may have done in the past. The truth is that, when you were involved with a sociopath, it's not that easy.

Work on your recovery

If you've had a devastating encounter with a sociopath, your top priority must be your personal recovery. Most likely, you have suffered not only heartbreak, but betrayal. Betrayal is very, very painful. Not only your feelings, but your sense of right and wrong, have been violated.

In order to move forward, you need to process the pain of the experience. This means allowing yourself to feel the pain however it presents to you — crying, groaning, pacing, putting your fist into a punching bag. We have lots of information on Lovefraud here to help you, both in the blog and in our webinars.

As you work through the pain of your involvement with the sociopath, you may find that it brings to mind other pain that you endured in the past. If this happens, it's good. Sociopaths hook us by latching onto internal pain from the past that we may not even be aware of. So if the sociopath rips the scab off of past traumas or betrayals, process them as well. The more you can get out of your system, the more prepared you will be to truly move forward.

Trying again

So how do you know if you are ready to date again? You'll feel reasonably centered. You are able to enjoy yourself. You have family and friends who care about you. Maybe your life isn't yet perfect, but it's moving in the right direction.

If you feel fearful or desperate about finding a partner, then you have more work to do.

The online ad

About the ad you found on Plenty of Fish — the guy sounds great. But is he telling the truth? When it comes to online ads, anyone can post anything; therefore, all dating profiles must be regarded with skepticism.

Let's analyze this ad. The guy says he's:

- Athletic body
- Easy going
- Romantic
- Loves outdoors, movies, travel
- Into running
- Loves animals
- Active in many charities
- Former Navy officer
- Traditional values
- Adventurous and open-minded
- Financially secure
- Looking to buy a home

Is it possible for someone to be like this? Yes. Is it possible that he is too good to be true? Yes. Is it possible that the ad was posted by a professional con man from Nigeria? Yes.

Maybe when you're feeling stronger, you'll be able to communicate with this person and evaluate whether he is what he says he is.

But Erica, you should not even be looking at online dating ads right now. Please first focus on your personal recovery.

Trust after betrayal by the sociopath

For everyone here at Lovefraud, there came a time when we could no longer continue in denial. We were forced to admit that someone we trusted had betrayed us. We felt devastation, anger, humiliation, grief and every other negative emotion on a therapy checklist.

We also berated ourselves for our naiveté, kicked ourselves for our gullibility, and castigated ourselves for trusting someone who shouldn't have been trusted. Overwhelmed by pain, we may have vowed that we would never trust again.

Hold on. As human beings, we need to trust. Human society is built on trust. The key is to determine who is trustworthy, and who is not.

Trust and human society

I wrote previously about Paul Zak's book, *The Moral Molecule*, in which he identified oxytocin, a neurotransmitter, as the key to human moral behavior. Read the Lovefraud Blog article, *Oxytocin, trust and why we fall for psychopaths*.

The foundation of Zak's theory is that human beings are supposed to trust. We are social animals. We were able to survive for millennia because we lived in groups, we cooperated and we helped each other. Trust is the glue that holds us together.

Zak started out as an economist, and then went on to study moral behavior. Here's a quote from his book that proves the importance of trust:

The level of trust in a society is the single most power-ful determinant of whether that society prospers or re-mains mired in poverty. Being able to enforce contracts, being able to rely on others to deliver what they promise and not cheat or steal, is a more powerful factor in a coun-try's economic development than education, access to re-sources—anything.

Trusting is normal. Trusting is healthy. So how can we make sure we trust appropriately?

Oxytocin and trust

Researchers have long known that oxytocin is released in the brain and bloodstream when we experience intimacy, especially during sex. We also are flooded with oxytocin during emotional intimacy, such as shared feelings, and physical touching, such as a hug.

But Zak found that oxytocin, which he calls the "Moral Mole-cule," is responsive to other interactions as well:

All you have to do to trigger this Moral Molecule is give someone a sign of trust. When one person extends himself to another in a trusting way, the person being trusted ex-periences a surge in oxytocin that makes her less likely to hold back, and less likely to cheat. Which is another way of saying that the feeling of being trusted makes a person more trustworthy.

Zak says that oxytocin inspires caring and generous behavior, at least in most people. It doesn't work in psychopaths. But oxy-tocin doesn't turn us all into starry-eyed do-gooders who cooperate with anybody. Rather, this neurotransmitter enables us to recognize and respond to the precise nature of human interac-tions. He says:

The Moral Molecule works like a gyroscope, helping us maintain our balance between behavior based on trust, and behavior based on wariness and distrust. In this way, oxytocin helps us navigate between the social benefits of openness, which are considerable, and the reasonable caution we need to avoid being taken for a ride.

Interfering with oxytocin

So how did we get taken for a ride? Why did we fall for someone who turned out to have no morals at all? Perhaps we weren't letting oxytocin do its job.

Zak doesn't spend a lot of time talking about psychopaths in his book. But he does relate the story of a devoutly religious prison guard who took pity on a convicted rapist. The prisoner said he'd found Jesus, and when he was paroled, the guard took him into his home. The prisoner raped and murdered the guard's daughter.

Here's the point, according to Zak:

> Distorted ideas from religion, just like distorted ideas from economics, or eugenics, can impair the ability of the Moral Molecule to do its job, which is not so much to make us "good" as to keep us in tune with our immediate environment in the most adaptive way.

At some point, the prison guard may have felt misgivings about bringing the convicted rapist into his home. But he was so invested in his religious convictions, and the promise of redemption, that he may have disregarded warnings or fear.

Intuition

In his book called *The Gift of Fear,* author Gavin DeBecker writes that the most powerful warning system we have is intuition. He says intuition evolved over millennia specifically to keep us safe from predators.

Usually, we ignore it.

To research my book, *Red Flags of Love Fraud — 10 signs you're dating a sociopath,* I invited Lovefraud readers to complete an Internet survey. One of my questions was, "In the beginning of the involvement, did you have a gut feeling or intuition that something wasn't right about the person or the relationship?" A whopping 71 percent of respondents answered "yes."

Why? Why did so many people ignore their intuition? Here were some reasons:

- 18 percent — Doubted themselves
- 12 percent — Gave the benefit of the doubt
- 11 percent — Questioned the sociopath, but accepted the answers
- 9 percent — Wanted to believe the sociopath

So almost three-quarters of the survey respondents instinctively knew there was something wrong with the person, but stayed anyway. We talked ourselves out of what our intuition told us.

Trusting ourselves

We have the tools to know who is trustworthy and who is not. Whether the source is oxytocin or intuition — or perhaps they're the same thing — we have internal knowing that can protect us. The key is to pay attention.

In order to trust others, we first must trust ourselves.

It may take us some time to rebuild, or develop, our self-trust. We need to recover from the sociopath. (Many articles on Lovefraud can help you with that.) We may need to release some beliefs, such as "there's good in everyone," or "anyone can be saved," that block our perception of warning signs.

Most people in the world can be trusted, but now we know there are exceptions. When we trust our own perceptions and intuition, we can accurately discern who deserves our trust, and who does not.

Know the truth: You are worthy

I received a very short email that asked a very important question. Here it is:

> Can you give me some advice on how to deal with people who proclaim that I'm worth nothing?

By way of background, the email came from a young woman whom we'll call "Alma."

You are worthy

Alma is a college student who first wrote to me back in January. A man who supervised her during her summer internship showed interest in her. Although the young woman initially did not respond, he pursued and pursued, until, thinking that he really loved her, Alma finally accepted him. Then, when she left the internship, the man dumped her.

Alma was traumatized and could not concentrate on her studies. But people around her thought that her devalue and discard was "nothing much."

In her recent email, Alma didn't provide any more information. But actually, that doesn't matter in answering her question.

External and internal

There are two aspects to dealing with someone who invalidates you: the external aspect and the internal aspect.

The external aspect is what Alma asked about — how do you deal with the people who say such a cruel and vicious thing to you?

The short answer is to remove them from your life. There is no point having any kind of involvement with people who tear you down.

Under their control

Now, this may be difficult if you are somehow under their control. Alma is young, and she may be referring to her parents, university professors, or work superiors. So let's look at each of these possibilities

Parents. Good parents love their children and do their best to nurture and support them. If you are trying your best in life (meaning you're not a criminal or a parasite), and a parent calls you worthless, then the parent is either a lousy parent or impaired — perhaps alcoholic or struggling with his or her own problems.

If your parent is impaired, you may want to back off of interactions with him or her until the problem is resolved. If you must have contact, build your emotional armor so that the hurtful statements bounce off of you.

If the parent has always said terrible things to you, and has also harmed you in other ways, you are justified in breaking off the relationship completely. Yes, we are supposed to honor our mother and father — but only if they're honorable.

University professors. University professors are supposed to teach students and prepare them for the future. But some professors have a mean streak. Or, they get caught up in academic politics.

The good news is that your time at the university will sooner or later be over. The bad news is that you may need a passing grade from the professor to graduate. If you can't transfer to another class, you may need to ignore the hurtful words and work really hard to get a good grade.

Know that the day will come when you will be out of there.

Work superiors. A supervisor or boss has no business making that kind of statement to an employee. But some people in the workplace are sociopathic bullies.

If you've been reading Lovefraud for a while, you know that once they are adults, sociopaths don't change. A mean boss will always be a mean boss. Therefore, the only reason to stay in that job is that you haven't yet found another job. Get out as soon as you can.

Friends and lovers

If someone who is supposed to be a friend says that you're worthless, well, that person is not a friend. Eliminate him or her from your life.

If it's your boyfriend, girlfriend or spouse who is saying these things, you need to evaluate the relationship.

Real love means supporting and caring about your partner. If you are trying your best in the relationship and in life, and your partner is tearing you down, then your partner is at best callous, and at worst sociopathic.

Sociopaths typically start relationships by lavishing you with love and attention, and then slowly morph their behavior into criticism and control. The criticism may first be over minor things like something that you cooked — but later escalate until it becomes really hurtful and damaging.

If your partner shows the key symptoms of a sociopath, know that tearing you down may be his or her objective. No matter what you do, you will never satisfy this person. To save yourself, you must get out of the relationship.

Internal aspect

The true solution to the problem of being called worthless is internal.

Know that you are worthy. Know that simply due to the fact that you are a living human being, you deserve to feel love, pursue happiness, and live your life in peace.

If you have any doubts about your worthiness, then you have internal healing to do.

It may help to determine where the doubts came from. Were you ever abused in any way? Did you receive negative messages from your parents, teachers, church or society while growing up?

Did small failures turn into big failures?

Maybe you experienced none of these things, but ideas of "less than" or "not good enough" still managed to take root in your brain. If that's the case, I suggest you sit quietly, with a pen and paper, and ask yourself what you feel.

An answer will percolate up from your subconscious. When you get your answer, ask why? When the next answer comes, again ask why? Keep going until you get to the root of the issue. You may be surprised at the beliefs that are hidden within you.

Real healing

Figuring out how the doubts began is a first step in the right direction. Real healing comes from releasing your negative experiences and beliefs.

How do you do that? In my experience, you allow yourself to feel the pain associated with them. In private or with the help of a qualified therapist, you bring the pain to mind and then let yourself cry, wail, yell in anger, stomp your feet — whatever you feel moved to do. You want to get the negative energy out of your system.

Then, replace the negative energy with positive energy. How? By doing anything that brings you joy and pleasure. Take a bubble bath. Walk your dog. Watch the sunset. Treat yourself to a chocolate chip cookie.

You may need to go through many rounds of releasing the negative and taking in the positive. But if you keep at it, eventually you will know the truth and truly believe it:

You are worthy, and anyone who says otherwise does not deserve to be in your life.

Love is always a leap of faith

Lovefraud received the following email from a reader with a request:

> I'm a huge fan of Lovefraud and can't thank you enough for making it happen. I know from your story that you've found a wonderful man. So have I, and we've been dating about a year. He's an upbeat, nurturing person with a great sense of humor and good boundaries!
>
> Still, I'm finding it difficult to let go and love him. I'm really surprised how long it's taking me to let go of my fear. (I've been out of my marriage 4 years and did a lot of healing before I met new guy.)
>
> Could you address this in one of your articles? I see a lot of info on how to recover, and how to spot a spath so you don't hook up with another one. But what about when you find a good guy? I'd love to hear about other people's experiences, how long it took them to relax into love, and anything they did to facilitate the process.

First of all, I am very glad that you have found someone special. So let's address the situation that you've brought up — letting go of fear so that you can fully enjoy your new relationship.

Here's the most important concept to understand: The key to finding and enjoying a good, healthy relationship always lies within ourselves.

If you're still feeling fear about the new relationship, it means that you have more healing to do. This is not a bad thing. Keep in mind that when it comes to our emotional lives, another word for "healing" is "growth." So as you move forward, you're getting to the deeper issues that may still stand in the way of emotional fulfillment. When you address them, you grow.

Whatever you've been doing to get to where you are now, keep doing it, focusing on the last remnants of the fear that you feel:

If you've been working with a therapist, ask him or her to help you.

If you've been journaling, ask yourself what you're afraid of, and write the answers.

If you've been processing your emotions, allow yourself to feel the fear, until it is released.

If you've been meditating, focus on the fear, and let the cause come into your awareness.

If you've been using EFT tapping, state the fear as the problem you want to resolve.

Emotional growth is a lifelong process. All relationships are opportunities for growth.

Interim steps

Sometimes there are interim steps between getting rid of the sociopath and finding a true life partner.

If you've read my first book, *Love Fraud,* you may remember that I started dating a man, John, seven months after I left my sociopathic husband. John was a normal, affectionate, caring man. We had a lot of fun, and I truly felt love with him.

The relationship ended 10 months later. Quite frankly, the end of that relationship hurt more than the end of my marriage. My ex-husband had betrayed me. I grieved the loss of my money, stability and self-esteem. But I no longer loved him; I was glad to get rid of him. When John and I broke up, I was heartbroken. We did share a love, and it was gone.

Eventually I realized that my relationship with John was never meant to be permanent. We were both taking the initial tentative steps out of emotional disappointment. We cared for each other and supported each other for almost a year, and then it was time for both of us to move on.

Our partner's problems

Even with Terry, who is now my husband, there was a time about a year into our relationship when it almost came apart. The problem wasn't our relationship, but other issues in Terry's life that made him feel like he couldn't continue.

Sociopaths, of course, often have problems in their lives. So how do we tell the difference between a healthy person with a problem, who deserves our love and support, and a sociopath who will be an unending source of turmoil?

The difference is that when a sociopath has a problem, we'll feel manipulated, deceived or bullied into fixing it. When a healthy person has a problem, we won't feel used when we're offering support.

I knew that Terry had to face his issues. I hoped that we'd be able to stay together, but there was a chance that our relationship would end. I knew that if that happened, it wasn't because I was deficient. I'd be unhappy, but I'd eventually pick myself up and start again.

Always risk

Keep in mind that there's always risk involved in entering a relationship, whether or not you were previously betrayed by a sociopath, and even if the other person is relatively healthy. When you reveal the contents of your heart, there is a chance that your feelings may not be reciprocated and you'll end up with a broken heart. In short, that's life.

If a relationship doesn't work out, it doesn't mean that there is something wrong with you. It may mean that you and the other person were only meant to travel together for a short time. It may also mean that the person was just a stepping stone to the real love of your life.

Love is a leap of faith. As you heal, you'll be able to find the courage to make the leap.

19 New Year's resolutions to help you recover from narcissistic abuse

The New Year is always a good time for new beginnings. If your wish for the New Year is to heal from a destructive relationship with a sociopath and recover from the narcissistic abuse that you endured, here are 19 resolutions to help you in 2019.

1. I will have No Contact with the sociopath — I will not call, text or send email, and I certainly won't meet him/her in person.
2. If the sociopath contacts me, I will not respond.
3. I will not try to get information about the sociopath from others.
4. I will not follow or stalk the sociopath on social media.
5. I will remember that anything the sociopath says could be a lie.
6. I will not try to prove myself to the sociopath (because anything he/she says about me is a lie).
7. Even though the sociopath tried to get me to doubt myself, I will trust my own perceptions.
8. I will not discuss my personal situation with anyone who knows the sociopath, because I don't want any information about me divulged.
9. I will memorize noncommittal canned answers so I can respond to any inquiries about the sociopath without becoming upset.

10. I will allow myself to cry, sob and grieve in private, or with a trusted therapist, because I know I need to process the pain of my experience.
11. Although obsession is a normal phase of recovery, I will gradually limit the time that I allow myself to obsess.
12. I accept that the sociopath never loved me, because he/she is incapable of loving anyone.
13. I accept that the person I thought I was involved with does not exist.
14. I accept that the sociopath betrayed me and intentionally engaged in narcissistic abuse.
15. I accept that the sociopath will never change.
16. I will give myself time and permission to heal from the narcissistic abuse.
17. I will be gentle with myself.
18. I will recognize that the sociopath took advantage of my humanity and I have nothing to be ashamed of.
19. I will remember that, no matter what the sociopath said or did, I am worthy of respect and love.

In order to truly recover from narcissistic abuse, you'll need to commit to your own healing. That means deciding that you want to feel better, and doing the internal work to accomplish your goal.

It can be a bumpy ride. As you process the emotions related to your involvement with the sociopath, you'll probably find that they are connected to previous emotions that made you vulnerable in the first place. For example, you may be crying about something the sociopath did, and then realize you are also crying about a similar experience with an earlier relationship or in your family of origin.

When this happens, recognize that you are making real progress. Your objective is to release any internal pain you may be carrying around, whether it is new or old. That is how you will truly recover.

A Lovefraud reader's happy ending

More than a year ago, Lovefraud heard from a reader whom we called "Rochelle." After 30 years, she'd reconnected with the first boy she ever loved. It felt like her chance to finally have the love she always wanted.

Except that the boy, now a man, was a sociopath, and the love was a mirage. Rochelle knew he was disordered, but still she pined for him. She asked, "When does it get to the point where he stops taking up space in my brain?"

Well, I just received another letter from Rochelle, and she has good news.

Dear Donna—

I was married to a sociopath, and had written to you when I was devastated by the aftermath of my divorce. I was diagnosed with breast cancer the same day my divorce became final. I read your books, followed the rules. I had slipped once and we had started "dating." That did not last long and I wrote him off completely. I kept reading your books and logging into Lovefraud. As time went on, I began dating, but I wasn't really thrilled.

One night, I went with a girlfriend to listen to music at a local club. It was a band I had seen before (with the ex) that I really enjoyed. My ex was a former singer and wanted to join this band. When they wanted nothing to do with him, we stopped going to see them, but I enjoyed their music. My girlfriend kept pointing out the saxophone player to me (she did it 4 times during the course of the evening!). I did something VERY uncharacteristic of my normal behavior. After the show, I approached him and told him how much I enjoyed his music. We started talking, and I gave him my business card. I was very cautious, and a little optimistic. We met for drinks during the following week, and talked about a lot of things. He was recently divorced after over 30 years of marriage. We swapped stories, and as time went on, we began dating and got closer. Slowly, I began to trust. We fell in love and have been together ever since.

I've learned so much from you and everything I've read. I studied the Red Flags. I looked for signs; there were none. I can tell you this relationship is...well....easy. No stress, no drama, no arguing or fighting. We compromise. We have a great time together....so much so that we moved in together. I kept my apartment for 6 months after moving in with him and finally moved in officially. He literally took the pieces of me and helped to put me back together. I feel whole again, physically and emotionally. You played a big role in that and I just wanted to thank you.

"Rochelle"

I asked Rochelle for permission to post her letter. Her story is evidence that yes, when you focus on recovery, there can be life, joy, happiness and love after the sociopath.

About the author

Donna Andersen is author of Lovefraud.com, a website that teaches people to recognize and recover from sociopaths. She is also author of *Red Flags of Love Fraud — 10 signs you're dating a sociopath* and the *Red Flags of Love Fraud Workbook*.

Donna learned about sociopaths the hard way — by marrying one. She tells the whole outrageous story in her first book, *Love Fraud — How marriage to a sociopath fulfilled my spiritual plan*. The book was awarded five stars by the Midwest Book Review.

Donna founded Lovefraud Education and Recovery. The non-profit offers online webinars to help professionals and the public spot, escape and recover from narcissists, antisocials, psychopaths and other manipulators. She is co-author of a scientific paper about therapy for victims of sociopaths, and has presented research to the Society for the Scientific Study of Psychopathy.

Donna has appeared on television shows including *Insight* in Australia, *ABC News 20/20, Who the Bleep Did I Marry?, My Life is a Lifetime Movie, Handsome Devils* and *The Ricki Lake Show*. She has been interviewed for multiple radio shows, print articles and web posts.

Donna graduated summa cum laude from the Syracuse University with degrees in magazine journalism and psychology. She was the original editor of Atlantic City Magazine, and then founded a boutique advertising agency, Donna Andersen Copywriting, in 1983. Her portfolio includes multimedia scriptwriting, freelance magazine articles, newsletters, web content and more.

Donna is happily remarried, proving that recovery from betrayal is possible.

30874690R00117